The CONTENTED LITTLE BABY

BOOK

OF

NAMES

The CONTENTED LITTLE BABY

BOOK

OF

NAMES

Over 3,000 names

Compiled by Gillian Delaforce

VERMILION
LONDON

7 9 10 8 6

First published in the United Kingdom in 1999 by Vermilion
an imprint of Ebury Press
Random House
20 Vauxhall Bridge Road · London SW1V 2SA

Random House Australia (Pty) Limited
20 Alfred Street · Milsons Point · Sydney · New South Wales 2061 · Australia

Random House New Zealand Limited
18 Poland Road · Glenfield · Auckland 10 · New Zealand

Random House South Africa (Pty) Limited
Endulini, 5A Jubilee Road · Parktown 2193 · South Africa

The Random House Group Limited Reg. No. 954009
www.randomhouse.co.uk

A CIP catalogue record for this book is available from the British Library

ISBN 0 09 182750 7

Printed and bound in Great Britain by Mackays of Chatham PLC, Chatham, Kent

Contents

Introduction

'What's in a name?' Shakespeare may have thought that a rose would smell as sweet by any other name but what we are called is enormously important. It affects our image and therefore it is vital that parents take care in choosing names for their children. After all, your name stays with you for your whole life. The right one can contribute to personal and professional success while the wrong one can lead to a lifetime of unhappiness.

There are many reasons for choosing a name. Often first names are handed down from generation to generation: in my own family the eldest son is given the name John and no other, which led to confusion when there were three generations with exactly the same names and initials. Sometimes parents choose a name to honour an elderly relation – perhaps in the hope that Great Aunt Ermintrude will remember the child in her will; or they use the mother's maiden name; or simply a word that has a pleasing sound to it. Fashions change and it is often possible approximately to guess someone's birthdate by their name; whole classes at school will have several children with the same name in a given era. When I was at school there were five of us with the same name in my class, so we were known by our initials. It used to be possible to tell a child's background from their name, but now names are interchangeable from the highest to the lowest in the land and there is not so much opportunity for snobbishness. In the same way as clothes, fashions in names recur; witness the recent popularity of Victorian names such as Amy and Emma. Nowadays, some of the major sources of modern names are television and films; as people see the same characters night after night on the screen inevitably the names of many these characters get passed on to their children.

RELIGION

Amongst Christians, Jews and Hindus the oldest traditional names come from the characters in the holy texts. Names such as Adam and Eve, Abigail and Ruth, Ganesh and Krishna, and the Apostles Peter, James, Matthew, Mark, Luke and John are always popular. Perhaps the most enduring female name is Mary, after the mother of Jesus, and this is followed closely by Rebecca and Sarah.

Many religious people, particularly Catholics, are eager to name their children after the early Christian martyrs, ascetics and mystics who have been canonized. St Francis of Assisi, patron saint of ecology; St Christopher, the patron saint of travellers, whose medal hangs around many necks to ensure safe journeys; St Bernadette, whose vision of the Virgin Mary led to the foundation of the shrine at Lourdes; and St Benedict who founded the Benedictine Order of monks are among the many saints whose names have been given to generations of children.

The majority of saints have been male, with the feminine versions of their names coming later, such as Frances and Georgina (for the patron saint of England, St George). Saints' names are listed separately at the back of the book for the benefit of parents who would like to follow this tradition.

The pagan early Roman names such as Claudius and Julius are rarely found nowadays, no doubt due to the attempts of the Christian church of the time to suppress all classical literature as being irreligious. However, the feminine form of those names have survived.

SURNAMES AND PLACENAMES

Surnames used as first names are more common in the US, probably because of the tradition of naming a child with the mother's maiden name. The problem with that is no one is quite sure whether you are male or female. Nelson, after Horatio Lord Nelson, and Cecil, after the aristocratic family, are examples of surnames used as first names in Britain.

Placenames tend to be more common among Afro-Americans; one example is the cricketer, Devon Malcolm. India is used as a female first name and was given to one of Lord Mountbatten's granddaughters in memory of his time as Viceroy of the sub-continent. There are also middle-aged women who have been called by the names of lakes and places in Kashmir where their fathers were serving in the army and Colonial Service. Often children will be given the name of the place where their parents are sure that they were conceived, a famous recent example being Brooklyn Beckham.

ROYALTY

Over the ages the names of kings, queens and princes have been popular first names. Elizabeth, borne by two long-reigning English queens, and George, borne by many English and European monarchs, have long been favourites. Edward, Charles and William, the names of the younger English royal princes, originally were Latin names which were translated into German and then Norman French before ending up in their current form. The names of the Old English kings, like Alfred, Ethelred and Edwin, and of the Old English queens, Elfreda and Boadiccea now seem rather old-fashioned to the modern parent. In the US Duke, Earl and King remain popular.

LANDS AND LEGENDS

Many of the names in this book come from Greek words, very often transmuted through Latin. The classic tradition is very strong, although the names of the Greek gods and goddesses such as Adonis, Aphrodite and Hero are not much found in the English-speaking world. Derivations from Irish or Scottish Gaelic are found world-wide: Bridget, Duncan, Ian and Sheila, or from Welsh Gareth, Gwendolyn and Trevor. There are Anglicized forms of Celtic names, such as Brendan, Cormac and Declan from the Gaelic and Dylan, Dilys, Olwen and Wyn from Welsh. In Scotland some names are associated with certain clans, so the Anglicized Sorley (Somhairle) is given to members of the Macdonald clan, and the name itself has Norse origins. The legendary court of King Arthur gave rise to many Welsh names, for instance Elaine, Lancelot, Merlin, Percival and Tristan.

LITERATURE, SPORT AND ENTERTAINMENT

Literary names influenced by famous plays or novels are not found as frequently as they were: Shakespeare's plays have not spawned a wealth of Cleopatras, Othellos and Desdemonas, although Helena, Olivia and even Portia are not uncommon. Fictional characters in films and television and the names of the actors and actresses who play them will always remain popular, such as Kylie from 'Neighbours'. Pop and rock music stars are also useful sources of names, witness the rise (and fall) of Madonna and Liam and no doubt there will be many little Geris, Mels and Emmas in the classrooms of tomorrow. For boys, the names of the sports stars of the day will always be a source of inspiration.

NATURE

Since the 19th century the names of rare and precious stones have been used as first names for girls – Beryl, Pearl, Ruby and less often Amber, Crystal and Jade. Flower names such as Daisy, Iris, Primrose and Violet are considered to be somewhat maiden-aunt-like, but Briony or Poppy are now more popular.

In some cultures, such as the Arabic, names are taken from any ordinary word, just for the sound of it and as parents seek to be innovative so they use words not traditionally associated with names, such as Moon, Sky or River.

SHORTFORMS AND NICKNAMES

You can't escape from the fact that people love to shorten names so it is important when choosing one to bear in mind what the diminutive might be. For example, while you might like the name Joseph, it is worth remembering that it is almost always shortened to Joe. However, shortforms can also work in your favour and many parents choose a name specifically for its shortform. Elly for Eleanor, being an example of this. Short forms, such as Reg, Dick or Bill, can be used in their own right and some parents use these on the birth registation form, but it is preferable to register the full name and so allow the child to choose their own variation in time. In the US, shortforms such as Bobby and Pam are particularly popular and it is customary there to put the shortform and not the longer version of the name on the birth certificate.

PITFALLS

There are various pitfalls to watch out for when thinking of names for your new baby. Initials are very important – you don't want their wallet or suitcase to spell out MAD, BAD or ASS. Neither do you want all your children to have the same initials; it is important for a child to have his or her own identity, not to mention the problems this will cause later at school. Equally, you don't want their first name added to your surname to make an unfortunate combination such as Ann Teake. A balance of a short first name with a long surname or of an unusual first name with a more common surname or vice versa makes for a pleasant sound. Another fact that is often forgotten is that your tiny baby will one day become an adult so it is important to imagine how a name will suit your child later on. Do you imagine your son will enjoy being called Timmy when he is a high-flying MD? It is also better to avoid names that give no clue as to the sex of the child; again, this is a question of identity.

There is a fashion in names as *The Times* list of the top ten names for each year shows (see opposite) so if you don't want your child to end up with the same name as half the other children in his or her class, then choose an alternative. However, care should be taken that the name chosen is not too unusual. Your child may not like it and other children can be cruel when faced with something 'different'. A friend of mine named his son Peregrine, but from the age of six the boy refused to be called by his first name and used his second name instead. A valuable lesson here is if you do choose an unusual first name, be sure to balance it with a more usual second name so that your child can make a choice later on.

TWINS AND TRIPLETS

Naming twins and triplets can be a problem. Do you give them all names with the same initial? Although this is tempting it is probably better avoided as it can cause confusion at school and on occasions when only initials are used. Also names that sound similar like Kristen and Christine and rhyming names like Pam and Sam can be a source of problems at school. Obviously paired names like Jack and Jill or Bill and Ben will lead to much teasing. For girl triplets flower names are an option – Jasmine, Lily and Rose for instance. Or the names of precious stones – Emerald, Sapphire and Pearl. Or perhaps Faith, Hope and Charity. But although these might sound attractive to the parents the children could easily be deeply resentful of such clichés. Boy twins or triplets can be given the names of favourite sporting stars or rock stars, but this does date them. One option is to keep to names with the same syllable: either one syllable like Tom and Pat; two like Andrew, Matthew and Janet; or three like Amanda, Clarissa and Nicholas. Another option is to name twins or triplets in reverse alphabetical order, so that the first-born is Richard and the second Adam. That way Adam will come first in something, which could be very important as he grows up.

Naming a child should be an enjoyable and positive experience. I hope the lists that follow will provide you with a plethora of ideas. Just remember the possible pitfalls and take your time. Good luck!

THE TIMES' LIST OF THE
TOP TEN NAMES FOR GIRLS AND BOYS
FOR 1998

The top ten boys' names

1. Thomas
2. William
3. James
4. Harry
5. Charles
6. Oliver
7. Alexander
8. George
9. Edward
10. Benjamin

Top ten girls' names

1. Olivia
2. Lucy
3. Isabel
4. Charlotte
5. Emily
6. Alice
7. Alexandra
8. Sophie
9. Isabella
10. Imogen

A ~ Girls

Abbie
A short form of Abigail.

Abigail
From the Hebrew, 'father of joy'. A popular name in the 16th and 17th centuries, it became used as a term for ladies' maids.
SHORT FORMS: Abbey, Abby, Gail, Gale.

Abilene
Possibly from the Hebrew, 'grass'. In the Bible this is a region in the Holy Land. This name is mainly used in the US.

Abira
From the Hebrew, 'strong, heroic'.
OTHER FORMS: Adira, Amiza.

Abra
The female form of Abraham, this name means 'mother of multitudes'.

Acacia
Of Greek origin, this is the name of a flower. It is a symbol of immortality.
SHORT FORMS: Cacia, Casey, Casia, Kacie.

Acantha
From the Greek, 'thorny'. The acanthus was used as a decorative form in Greek architecture.

Accalia
A character in Roman mythology, supposed to be foster-mother of Romulus and Remus.

Ada
From the Old German, 'noble', this is a short form of Adela or Adelaide.
OTHER FORMS: Addie, Aida, Eda, Edna.

Adabelle
A modern combination of Ada and Belle.

Adah
From the Hebrew, 'beauty, ornament'. This is one of the earliest recorded Hebrew names.
SHORT FORMS: Ada, Adie, Adina, Dina.

Adalind
A variation of Adelaide.

Adaline
A variation of Adelaide.

Adamina
The female form of Adam.

Adar
From the Hebrew, 'fire'.

Adara
From the Arabic, 'virgin'.

Adela
From the Old German, 'noble'. A popular name in the reign of Queen Victoria .
SHORT FORMS: Addie, Adel, Del, Della, Edila.

Adelaide
The French form from the Old German for 'noble' and 'sort'. The name became popular in the 19th century due to Queen Adelaide, wife of William IV of England.
OTHER FORMS: Adalia, Addi, Adelina, Adeliz, Heida.

Adelinda
A combination of Adel and Linda.

Adeline
Also from the Old German, 'noble', it was brought to England by the Normans.
OTHER FORMS: Ada, Adelena, Aline.

Adelpha
From the Greek, 'sister', 'sister to mankind'.

Aderyn
From the Welsh, 'bird'.

Adesina
This name comes from Nigeria and is used by the Yoruba tribe for children of previously childless mothers.

Adiel
From the Hebrew, 'ornament of the Lord'.
OTHER FORMS: Adie, Adiell, Adiella.

Aditi
An Indian name, from the Sanskrit meaning 'abundant creative power'.

Adolpha
The female form of Adolph.
OTHER FORM: Adolpham.

Adonia
Female form of Adonis, meaning 'beautiful woman'.

Adora
From the Latin and French meaning 'worthy of divine worship'.
OTHER FORMS: Adoria, Dora, Dorie, Dury.

Adorna
From the Middle English, 'beautify, embellish'.

Adria
A variation of Adrienne.

Adriana
An Italian female form of Adrian.

Adrianne
A variation of Adrienne.

Adrienne
From the Greek and Latin, 'rich' and 'black, mysterious'. This name is often given to girls with dark hair and eyes.
OTHER FORMS: Adrien, Adrina, Hadria.

Affrica
This name is Anglo-Saxon, meaning 'beloved, free'. In the 12th century Affrica was wife of Semerled, King of the Isle of Man.

Afra
From the Hebrew, 'young female deer'.
OTHER FORMS: Aphra, Aphrah, Ayfara.

Agata
A variation of Agatha.

Agate
From Old French and Greek, 'precious stone'. In the 16th century small figures were cut into agate, leading to the name signifying a diminutive person.

Agatha
Female form of the Greek, meaning 'good, kind woman'. St. Agatha was a Sicilian Christian martyr.
SHORT FORMS: Ag, Agase, Aggi, Atka.

Aggie
A short form of Agatha, also used in its own right.

Aglaia
From the Greek, 'splendid, brilliant'. Aglaia was one of the Three Graces, who presided over the rebirth of nature in spring and the ripening of fruit in autumn.

Agnes
From the Greek, 'pure, chaste'. There were two saints called Agnes, one was martyred in Rome in the 3rd century and the other came from Tuscany.
SHORT FORMS: Aggy, Annais, Annice, Anis, Inez, Nesta.

Aharona

Female form of Aaron.

SHORT FORMS: Arni, Arnina, Arona.

Ahimsa

In Hindi this means reverence for life and belief in peaceful solutions to problems.

Ahulani

Hawaiian for 'heavenly shrine'.

Aida

From the French, 'to help, assist'. In Verdi's opera Aida is an Ethiopian princess who dies to save her people.

OTHER FORMS: Aidan, Iraida, Zaida, Zenaida, Zoraida.

Ailene

Irish, from the Greek, 'light'.

OTHER FORMS: Aila, Aileen, Ileane, Lena.

Ailsa

This name comes from Ailsa Craig, a Scottish island.

Aimee

The French form of Amy, often spelt with an accent on the first 'e'.

Aisha

From the Arabic, meaning 'prospering'.

OTHER FORMS; Aiesha, Aishal, Asia.

Aisling

From the Gaelic, 'dream, vision'.

OTHER FORMS: Aislinn, Ashling, Isleen.

Aithne

From the Celtic, 'little fire'. A popular name in Ireland, it was used for a goddess and a number of queens and saints.

SHORT FORMS: Aine, Eithne, Ena, Ethne.

Akako

Japanese, meaning 'red'.

Alaina

Female form of Alan.

OTHER FORMS: Alana, Alina, Allene, Alanna, Lan(n)a.

Alameda

From the Spanish, 'poplar tree'.

Alaula

Hawaiian, meaning 'dawn light' and 'sunset glow'.

Alberta

Female form of Albert, which comes from the German, 'noble and bright'. It was very popular in Victorian times, in honour of Prince Albert.

OTHER FORMS: Albertha, Alli, Allie, Berta.

Albertina

A diminutive of Alberta.

Albertine

A variation of Albertina and the name of a climbing rose.

Albina

From the Latin, 'white'. A good choice for blonde girls.
OTHER FORMS: Albinia, Alvinia, Aubine.

Alathea

From the Greek, 'truth'. This name was introduced to England from Spain in the 17th century.
OTHER FORMS: Aleta, Letitia, Letty.

Aletta

A short form of Alathea.

Alex

A short form of Alexandra or Alexis, used in its own right.

Alexandra

Female form of Alexander. Many of the Royal Family have been given this name.
SHORT FORMS: Alexa, Lexie, Sacha, Sandra, Zandra.

Alexis

From the Greek, 'helper'. The name of an Orthodox Greek saint, this was originally a boy's name but is now frequently used for girls.
OTHER FORMS: Alexa, Alexia.

Alice

From the Old German, 'noble', it was originally Adelice or Adelise. It became very popular in the 19th century after 'Alice in Wonderland' (Lewis Carroll) was published.
OTHER FORMS: Ailis, Alix, Alli, Alys.

Alicia

A variation of Alice.

Alida

From the German, 'noble and kind', this is a Hungarian short form of Adelaide.

Alima

From the Arabic, 'learned in music and dancing'.

Aline

This can be pronounced in the French way with a short 'a' or in the English with a long 'a'. Originally a short form of Adeline.
OTHER FORM: Alina.

Alison

Originally this was another form of Alice but is now used as a separate name.
OTHER FORMS: Allison, Alyson.

Alissa

A variation of Alicia.

Aliya

From the Hebrew, 'to ascend, rise up'.

Allegra

Italian for 'cheerful, lively'. This name was given to Lord Byron's daughter.

Allice

A variation of Alice.

Allie

A short form of Alice or Alison.

Allyce

A variation of Alice.

Alma

Derived from the Hebrew, 'maiden' and the Latin, 'kind', this name became popular after the Battle of Alma in the Crimean War.

Aloha

Hawaiian greeting, conveying warmth and kindness.

Althea

From the Greek, 'wholesome, healthy', this was the name for the marsh mallow plant, which is still used for healing purposes.
OTHER FORM: Altheda

Alvina

A variation of Albina.

Alyce

A variation of Alice.

Alys

A variation of Alice.
OTHER FORM: Alyssa.

Alyson

A variation of Alison.
OTHER FORMS: Alysson.

Alyx

A short form of Alexandra and a variation of Alice.

Amabel

From the Latin, 'lovable'.
SHORT FORMS: Bel, Belle, Mabel.

Amalia

A variation of Amelia.
OTHER FORM: Amalie.

Amaline

A variation of Amelia.

Amalita

A variation of Amelia.

Amanda

From the Latin, 'worthy of love'. Fashionable during the Restoration it was also used by Noel Coward in his play 'Private Lives'.
SHORT FORMS: Manda, Mandi(e), Mandy.

Amaryllis

From the Greek, 'sparkling', this is the name of a lily.

Amber

From the Arabic, this a deep yellow resin used for jewellery.
OTHER FORMS: Amberlie, Amby

Ambrin

From the Arabic word for 'ambergris'.

Ambrosia

From the Greek, 'elixir of life'. It was the mythical food of the gods.

Ambrosina

A variation of Ambrosia.
OTHER FORM: Ambrosine.

Amelia

From the Latin, 'toil, work', this name was introduced from Germany.
SHORT FORMS: Amy, Emily, Milly.

Amethyst

From the Greek, 'intoxicated', this is a violet-coloured precious stone.

Amie

A variation of Amy.

Amina

Female form of Amin, from the Arabic, 'honest'.
OTHER FORMS: Aamenha, Amena.

Amira

From the Arabic, 'princess'.

Aminta

From the Latin, 'protector'.

Amity

From the Latin, 'friendship'.

Amy

From the French, 'love'.
OTHER FORMS: Ami, Amie, Amye.

Anäis

A French name, taken from the Greek, 'fruitful'.

Ananda

From the Sanskrit, 'happiness', it is the name of a god in the *Veda*.
OTHER FORMS: Anandi, Andini.

Anchoret

From the Welsh, 'much loved'.

Ancret

A variation of Angharad.

Andrea

Female form of Andrew.
SHORT FORMS: Andi, Andram, Andy.

Aneka

A variation of Anneka or Anneke.

Anemone

From the Greek, 'wind-flower', the name of a flower grown in Britain.

Angela

From the Latin, 'angelus', derived from the Greek, 'messenger'.
OTHER FORMS: Angel, Angelica, Angelique, Angie.

Angelica

French, 'like an angel'.
OTHER FORMS: Angelika, Angelita.

Angharad

Welsh for 'much loved', the stress is on the second syllable.
OTHER FORMS: Ancrett, Angahard.

Anila

A Sanskrit name, the female form of Anil.

Anisha

One of the thousand names of the Hindu god, Vishnu.

Anna

Greek form of Hannah.
OTHER FORMS: Ana, Anett, Nan, Nana.

Annabel

This may derive from Amabel and is popular in Scotland.
OTHER FORMS: Annabella, Bel, Belle, Bella.

Anne

French form of Hannah, meaning 'God has favoured me'.
OTHER FORMS: Ann, Annie, Anya.

Anneka

A Dutch pet form of Ann.
OTHER FORM: Anneke.

Annes

A variation of Agnes.

Annette
A variation of Anne.

Annice
A variation of Agnes.

Annis
A variation of Agnes.

Anita
A variation of Anne.

Annunciata
From the Latin, 'bearer of news', this comes from the Annunciation to the Virgin Mary.
SHORT FORM: Nunciata.

Anona
From the Latin, 'annual crops'. She was the Roman goddess of crops.

Anora
A variation of Honora or Honoria.

Anouk
The Slav form of Anne.

Anthea
From the Greek, 'flowery'.
SHORT FORM: Anthia

Antoinette
Female form of Anthony. The name of a French queen, Marie Antoinette and of several saints.
OTHER FORMS: Net(tie), Tanya, Toinette, Toni.

Anusha
The Hindu name of an astral star.

Anya
The Russian form of Anne.

Aoife
From the Gaelic, 'radiant', this is the Irish form of Eve.

Aphrodite
From the Greek, 'born of foam', she was the most beautiful goddess of all.

April
The name signifies springtime, from the Latin, 'open to the sun'.
OTHER FORMS: Averil, Averyl, Avril.

Arabella
Either from the German, 'eagle', or the Latin, 'altar', plus 'beautiful'.
SHORT FORMS: Ara, Arbell, Bella, Belle.

Araminta

A name that was probably invented in the 17th century by Sir John Vanbrugh.

SHORT FORMS: Minta, Minty.

Aretha

Greek for 'virtue', this has become known through the singer of the same name.

Argenta

From the Latin, 'silver'.

Ariadne

From the Greek, 'very divine', she was a princess in mythology.

OTHER FORMS: Ariana, Ariane, Arianna.

Arianwen

From the Welsh, 'silver'.

Ariel

A popular name in the US, it was used by Shakespeare for an airy spirit.

OTHER FORMS: Arial, Ariela, Arielle.

Arleen

A modern coinage using the popular 'leen' ending.

Arlene

This is a modern name, with no special meaning.

OTHER FORM: Arline.

Arlette

Of French origin, this was the name of the mother of William the Conqueror.

Arminell

A female form of Herman.

OTHER FORM: Arminel.

Artemisia

Goddess of hunting and animals in Greek mythology.

SHORT FORMS: Arta, Arte, Artema.

Aruna

From the Sanskrit, 'dawn'.

OTHER FORM: Arumina

Ashleigh

This means 'ash field' and is taken from the name of a place.

OTHER FORMS: Ashlynn, Ashton.

Ashley

A popular variation of Ashleigh.

Asma

From the Arabic, 'more eminent'. Asma was the daughter of Abu-Bakr.

Asoka

An Indian name, famous for the great emperor of the Mauryan Empire.

SHORT FORMS: Ashok, Ashoka.

Aspen
A type of tree with delicate leaves. Popular in the US.

Asphodel
Greek for the lily family that includes daffodils and narcissus.

Astrid
Norse, from the Old German, 'god' and 'beauty'.
OTHER FORM: Astera.

Atalanta
From Greek mythology, she was a fast runner who said she would marry any man who could out-run her. The winner threw golden apples in her path and won the race when she stopped to pick them up.

Athene
Greek goddess of crafts, war and wisdom.
OTHER FORM: Athena

Audrey
A saint whose name is a short form of Ethelreda. The word 'tawdry' comes from the cheap necklaces sold at her festival.
OTHER FORMS: Addie, Audey, Audry, Awdrie.

Augusta
From the Latin, 'venerable'. Female form of Augustus, the name of a Roman emperor.
OTHER FORMS: Augustina, Gus, Gussie.

Aurelia
From the Latin, 'golden'.
SHORT FORMS: Auriol, Auriel, Oriel, Oriole.

Aurora
From the Latin, 'dawn'.
SHORT FORMS: Aurore, Ora, Rora, Rorie.

Ava
Made famous by the film star, Ava Gardner.

Averil
Probably from the Old English, 'boar' and 'battle'.

Avis
From the Old German, 'refuge in war', or the Latin, 'bird'.
OTHER FORMS: Aves, Avice, Avison.

Avril
The French for April, popular for girls born in that month.

Ayesha

A variation of Aisha.
OTHER FORMS: Ayisha, Aysha, Ayshia.

Azalea

Taken from the name of the scented colourful shrubs that bloom in the spring.
OTHER FORMS: Azalee, Azelea.

Azimah

From the Arabic, 'determined'.

Aziza

From the Arabic, 'beloved, dear', also Swahili, 'precious'.
OTHER FORM: Asisa

Azura

From the Persian, 'lapis lazuli', a rich blue precious stone.
OTHER FORMS: Azora, Azure, Azurine.

A ~ Boys

Aaron
This comes from the Hebrew, 'mountain'. Aaron was the brother of Moses and the first high priest of Israel.
SHORT FORMS: Ari, Arnie, Ron.

Abdullah
From the Arabic, 'servant of Allah'.
SHORT FORMS: Abdal, Abdul, Del.

Abel
Possibly from the Hebrew, 'son'. Abel was the second son of Adam and Eve.
SHORT FORMS: Abe, Abie, Able, Nab.

Abelard
One of the most famous lovers of history, who later became a monk.
SHORT FORMS: Ab, Abbey, Abby.

Abid
From the Arabic, 'servant'.

Abishai
From the Hebrew, 'my father's gift'. In the Bible he was a grandson of Jesse.
OTHER FORM: Abisha.

Abner
From the Hebrew, 'father of light', the name came to England in the early 16th century.
OTHER FORMS: Avner, Eb, Ebbie, Ebner.

Abraham
The first patriarch in the Bible, this name means 'eternal father' in Hebrew.
SHORT FORMS: Abe, Bram, Ham.

Abram
A variation of Abraham and shortform.

Absalom
From the Hebrew, 'father of peace'. Popular during the Middle Ages.
OTHER FORM: Absolum.

Acayid
From the Turkish, 'strange' or 'wonderful'.

Ace
From the Latin, ' a unit'.
OTHER FORMS: Acie, Ascie, Azzo.

Achilles

A valiant warrior in Greek mythology who only had one vulnerable spot, his heel.

OTHER FORMS: Achille, Achilleus.

Ackley

From the Middle English, 'acorn meadow'.

Acton

From the Old English, 'village with oak trees'. This is also from an English place name.

Adam

From the Hebrew, 'earth'. He was the first man created by God in the Garden of Eden.

SHORT FORMS: Ad, Adan, Addie, Adom, Edom.

Adar

From the Hebrew, 'dark and cloudy'.

OTHER FORMS: Addi(e), Adin, Adna, Ard(a).

Adlai

A biblical name, from the Hebrew, 'God is just'. Associated with the American statesman Adlai Stevenson.

Adler

From the German, 'eagle'.

Adolph

From the Old German, 'noble' and 'wolf'.

OTHER FORMS: Adolf, Adolphus, Dolph, Dolphus.

Adon

From the Hebrew, 'belonging to the Lord'. Adonai is another name for God.

Adonis

Originally a Phoenician word, via Greek, for 'lord'. The Greek god was very handsome and the name came to stand for male beauty.

Adrian

A British saint who was martyred in the 4th century.

OTHER FORMS: Ade, Adriano, Adrien, Hadrian.

Aeneas

A mythical character whose adventures are told by Virgil in *The Aeneid*.

SHORT FORMS: Angus, Eneas, Enne.

Ahearn

From the Gaelic, 'owner of horses'.

OTHER FORMS: Ahern(e), Hearn(e).

Ahmad

Arabic name meaning 'more praiseworthy'.
OTHER FORM: Ahmed

Aidan

From the Gaelic, 'little fiery one'. An Irish saint who founded the monastery at Lindisfarne.
OTHER FORMS: Edan, Eden.

Ainsley

Scottish for 'own place or field'.
OTHER FORM: Ainslie

Ajay

From the Sanskrit, 'invincible'.

Akash

From the Sanskrit, 'the sky'.
OTHER FORM: Aakash

Akshar

From the Sanskrit, 'imperishable'.

Alan

An old Celtic name, possibly meaning 'harmony'.
OTHER FORMS: Alain, Alein, Allan, Alun.

Alard

Old German, meaning 'tough and noble'.
OTHER FORMS: Adlard, Alart, Allard.

Alaric

Old German, meaning 'ruler over all'.
OTHER FORMS: Alarick, Alarik, Rich, Ricky.

Alastair

Gaelic form of Alexander, 'defender of men'.
SHORT FORMS: Al, Ali, Ally, Alec, Alick.

Alban

From the Latin, 'man from Alba', this is the name of the earliest British saint.
OTHER FORMS: Albin, Albinus, Alva, Elva.

Alberic

German, meaning 'powerful elf'. He is the king of the dwarfs in Wagner's *The Ring of the Nibelung*.
OTHER FORMS: Alberich, Auberon, Aubrey, Oberon.

Albert

Old German, meaning 'noble and bright'. Popular in Victorian times after Queen Victoria's Consort.
SHORT FORMS: Al, Albie, Bert, Bertie.

Aldous

Old German, meaning 'old', implying wisdom and maturity.
SHORT FORM: Aldo

Aldwyn
Anglo-Saxon, meaning 'old friend'.
OTHER FORMS: Aldan, Aldin, Aldwin.

Alec
This is a short form of Alastair and Alexander.

Aled
The name of a Welsh river.

Alexander
From the Greek, 'defender of men'. Most famous was Alexander the Great in the 4th century BC.
SHORT FORMS: Al, Alec, Alex, Ali, Sacha, Sandy.

Alexis
From the Greek, 'helper', he was one of the great Orthodox saints.
OTHER FORM: Alexie.

Alfred
Old English meaning 'good counsel'. Alfred the Great was King of Wessex in the 9th century.
SHORT FORMS: Alf, Alfie, Fred, Freddie.

Algernon
From the French, 'with whiskers'. Popular in the 19th century.
SHORT FORMS: Alger, Algie, Algy.

Ali
Popular Arabic name from the word meaning 'the god'.

Allan
A variation of Alan.

Allen
A variation of Alan.

Aloysius
Latin form of Aloys, from the French, Louis. There was a saint of this name in the 16th century.

Alwin
Old English meaning 'friend of all'.
OTHER FORMS: Alvan, Alvy, Alvyn, Aylwin.

Amadeus
The most famous bearer of the name was Wolfgang Amadeus Mozart.
SHORT FORMS: Amadis, Ama(n)do.

Ambrose
From the Greek, 'divine'. There was a 4th-century saint who was Bishop of Milan.
OTHER FORMS: Ambie, Ambros, Brose, Emrys.

Amin
From the Arabic, 'honest, reliable'.
OTHER FORMS: Amen, Amon, Ammon.

Amir

From the Arabic, 'prince'.
OTHER FORM: Emir

Amit

From the Sanskrit, 'without limit', it is also short for Amitbikram ('limitless prowess') and Amitjyoti ('limitless brightness').

Amitabh

A name for the Buddha, meaning 'limitless splendour'.
OTHER FORM: Amitav.

Amos

From the Hebrew, 'troubled', it was the name of an Old Testament prophet.

Amrit

From the Sanskrit, it refers to the 'water of life, nectar' or immortality.

Anand

The name of a god in the *Veda*, it means 'happiness' or 'joy'.
OTHER FORMS: Anandi, Anandini.

Anatole

From the Greek, 'rising sun'. Anatolia is the Asian part of Turkey.
SHORT FORMS: Anatol, Antal.

André

This is the French form of Andrew.

Andreas

The Greek form of Andrew.

Andrew

From the Greek, 'manly', this is the name of the patron saint of Scotland.
SHORT FORMS: Andra, Andy, Dandy, Drew.

Andy

A short form of Andrew, used as an independent name.

Aneurin

Welsh form of Honorius, 'honourable', this is one of the oldest names still used in Britain. The Labour politician, Aneurin Bevan, helped set up the National Health Service in Britain.
OTHER FORMS: Aneirin, Neirin, Nye.

Angus

From the Gaelic, 'one choice'. Common in Scotland, it also is the name of a breed of fine cattle.
SHORT FORMS: Ennis, Gus.

Anil

From the Sanskrit, 'air' or 'wind', he drives Indra's golden chariot in the Vedic epics.

Anish

One of the names of the Hindu god, Vishnu.

Antoine

The French form of Anthony.

Anthony

Possibly derived from the Greek, 'flourishing'. The name of Roman emperors and of saints.
OTHER FORMS: Anton, Tonio, Tony.

Antony

A variation of Anthony.

Anup

From the Sanskrit, 'without comparison'.
OTHER FORM: Anoop.

Apollo

Mythical god of the sun and light, possessing great charm and beauty.

Archibald

From the Old German, 'truly bold'. A favourite name in Scotland, particularly with the Campbell and Douglas clans.
SHORT FORMS: Archer, Archy, Arky.

Archie

A short form of Archibald, sometimes used in its own right.

Arden

From the Latin, 'to be on fire'.
SHORT FORMS: Ard, Arda, Ardie, Ardin.

Argus

From the Greek, 'highly observant'. The mythical giant with a hundred eyes, which were strewn on the tail feathers of the peacock after his death.

Ari

A short form of Ariel or of Aristotle.

Ariel

One of the Hebrew names for God, it is popular in Israel.
SHORT FORMS: Arie, Areli, Aryeh, Aryell.

Aristotle

From the Greek, 'best'. He was one of the greatest philosophers in the 4th century BC.
SHORT FORMS: Ari, Aristo.

Arjun

A Hindu name from the Sanskrit, 'white, bright'.

Armand

French form of Herman.
OTHER FORMS: Armando, Armine.

Armin
A variation of Herman.

Armon
From the Hebrew, 'castle' or 'palace'.

Arnold
From the Old German, 'eagle's power'. It had a revival in the late 19th and 20th centuries.
SHORT FORMS: Arn, Arnie, Arno.

Aron
A variation of Aaron.

Aroon
A variation of Arun.

Art
A short form of Arthur, used in its own right, particularly in the US.

Arthur
Possibly from the Celtic, 'bear'. Made famous by the 6th-century British King Arthur whose knights sat at the Round Table.
SHORT FORMS: Ard, Artie.

Arun
Sanskrit for 'reddish brown', signifying the dawn. The name was given to the sun's mythical charioteer.
OTHER FORM: Aroon.

Asa
From the Hebrew, 'physician', this name is particularly common to northern England.

Asaph
From the Hebrew, 'to gather'.

Ash
From the Old English, 'ash tree'. Also a short form of Ashley.

Asha
From the Sanskrit, 'hope'.

Asher
A biblical name for one of the tribes of Israel. from the Hebrew, 'happy'.
OTHER FORMS: Aser, Asser.

Ashley
This means 'ash field' and is now a popular name, particularly in the US.

Ashraf
From the Arabic, 'more noble, honourable'.

Ashton

From the Anglo-Saxon, 'dweller at the ash tree farm'.

SHORT FORM: Ash.

Athelstan

From the Old English, 'noble' and 'stone', this was the name of a king of Wessex.

Atlas

The mythical Greek giant who bore the world on his shoulders and was immensely strong.

Atilla

From the Greek, 'father'. Atilla the Hun fought the Romans in the 5th century.

Auberon

From an Old French name, possibly connected with Aubrey.

OTHER FORM: Oberon.

Aubrey

From the Old German, 'elf ruler'.

OTHER FORM: Alberic.

Audwin

From the German, 'noble friend'.

Augustine

The name of the saint who brought Christianity to Britain.

Augustus

From the Latin, 'venerable', this was the name of the first Roman emperor.

SHORT FORMS: August, Austyn, Austen, Gus, Gussie.

Aurelius

From the Latin, 'golden', this was the name of several early saints.

Austin

A short form of Augustine, but mostly used independently.

Averell

From the Anglo-Saxon for 'born in April' or 'like a boar'.

OTHER FORMS: Averil, Averill.

Axel

Scandinavian form of Absalom, from the Germanic 'oak'.

OTHER FORM: Aksel.

Aylmer

From the Old English, 'noble and famous'.

OTHER FORMS: Athel, Elmer.

Azaria

From the Hebrew, 'God is my help', this was the name of a king of Judah.

OTHER FORMS: Azarish, Azriel.

B ~ Girls

Babs
Short form of Barbara.

Bailey
This is a surname that comes from 'bailiff' or 'steward' and is fashionable in the US.

Bairn
From the Scottish, 'child'.

Bala
From the Sanskrit, 'young child'.

Barbara
From the Greek, 'strange' or 'foreign'. Barbara was a 3rd-century saint who is patron of architects, engineers and miners.
SHORT FORMS: Bab, Babette, Babs, Bobbi.

Barbie
A short form of Barbara, known from the Barbie doll.

Barbra
A modern short form of Barbara.

Bathsheba
From the Hebrew, 'daughter of opulence'. A biblical character, wife of Uriah and then of King David, she was the mother of Solomon.
OTHER FORMS: Bersaba, Sheba, Sheva.

Bea
A short form of Beata or Beatrice.

Beata
From the Latin, 'blessed' or 'happy'.

Beatrice
From the Latin, 'bearer of blessings'. The name was used by Dante and Shakespeare and is currently borne by one of the Royal princesses.
SHORT FORMS: Bea, Bee, Beatty, Trixie.

Beatrix
The Latinate form of Beatrice. It is the name of a 4th-century saint.

Beck
A modern short form of Rebecca.

Becky
A short form of Rebecca.

Bedelia
A variation of Bridget.

Béibhinn
A traditional Irish name meaning 'fair lady'.

Beige
Taken from the name of the colour, this is used mainly in the US.

Belinda
The first part of the name is from the Latin, 'beautiful' and the last part comes from Old German, and means 'a snake'. It was used in the poem *The Rape of the Lock*.
SHORT FORMS: Bel, Linda, Lindi, Lynde.

Bella
A short form of Arabella or Isabella.

Belle
A French form of Bella. The French for 'beautiful'.

Benedicta
Female form of Benedict, 'blessed one'.
OTHER FORMS: Bendetta, Benet, Betta, Binnie.

Benita
From the Spanish, 'blessed'.

Berenice
From the Greek, 'bringer of victory', it was widely known during the time of the Greek and Roman empires.
SHORT FORMS: Bernice, Bunny, Vernice.

Bernadette
The French female form of Bernard. St Bernadette saw a vision of the Virgin Mary at Lourdes, where pilgrims now go to be cured.

Bernice
A more modern variation of Berenice.

Bertha
From the Old German, 'bright', it was the name of Charlemagne's mother and also of the wife of King Ethelbert of Kent.
OTHER FORMS: Berta, Berte, Bird, Birdie.

Bertina
A variation of Bertha.

Beryl
A precious stone, which in Arabic means 'crystal' and in Greek means 'sea-green jewel'.
OTHER FORMS: Beruria, Berylla.

Bess, Bessie
Short forms of Elizabeth.

Beth
In Scotland this name comes from the Celtic, 'breath of life', as in Macbeth. It is also a short form of Elizabeth.

Bethany
This is the name of the village where Lazarus lived.
SHORT FORM: Bethan.

Bethia
Either a biblical place name, or a version of the Gaelic, 'life'.
OTHER FORM: Bethea.

Betsy
A short form of Elizabeth.

Bettina
An Italian form of Betty.

Betty
A short form of Elizabeth.

Beulah
From the Hebrew, 'married', this name was used for Israel in the Bible. In *The Pilgrim's Progress* it was the land of heavenly joy.

Beverley
Old English, meaning 'beaver's meadow'.
SHORT FORM: Bev.

Bharati
A Hindu name with connections to the goddess of learning and speech.

Bhavini
A Hindu name, after the goddess Parvati.

Bhavna
From the Sanskrit, 'wish' or 'thought'.
OTHER FORM: Bhavana.

Bianca
From the Italian, 'white'. Shakespeare used the name in two of his plays. Currently it is popular due to Bianca Jagger, the model and peace worker.

Biddy
An Anglo-Irish name, a pet form of Bridget. 'An old biddy' has come to mean 'a tiresome old woman'.

Billie
Female form of William. Also from the Old English, 'resolution'. Popular in the US.

Bina
A short form of Sabina.

Binnie

A pet form of Benedicta.

Birdie

A modern name taken from 'bird'.
OTHER FORMS: Birdella, Byrd, Byrdie.

Blair

From the Celtic, 'place, field'.
OTHER FORM: Blaire.

Blaise

A French name probably from the Latin, 'lisping'. Used for girls in the English-speaking world.

Blanche

A French name, from the word, 'white' or 'fair-skinned'.
OTHER FORMS: Bianca, Blanca, Blinni, Branca.

Blodwen

From the Welsh, 'white flower'.
OTHER FORMS: Blodeuwedd, Blodeyn.

Blossom

From the Old English, 'a plant or tree in flower'.
SHORT FORM: Bluma.

Bobbie

A variation of Bobby

Bobby

A pet name for Roberta and Barbara but it is used in its own right. Also used with other names, such as Bobby Anne.

Bonita

From the Spanish, 'pretty'.

Bonnie

Scots for 'pretty'. The name was used in *Gone with the Wind*.

Bonny

A variation of Bonnie.

Brandi

A popular name in the US, probably derived from the spirit, brandy.
OTHER FORMS: Brandee, Brandie.

Branwen

Traditional Welsh name, possibly meaning 'fair raven'.
OTHER FORM: Brangwen.

Breanna

A new name, which comes from the US, it is a blend of Bree and Anna.
OTHER FORMS: Breanne, Brieanne.

Brenda

Female form of Brendan or Brand, it is probably of Scandinavian origin.

Brenna

Feminine form of Bren or Brennan, this name mainly comes from the US.

Brianna

Female form of Brian, which is of Celtic origin.
OTHER FORM: Brianne.

Bridget

The Celtic goddess and an Irish saint, this name means 'strong, high'.
OTHER FORMS: Biddy, Brigit, Brigitta.

Bridgid

A variation of Bridget.

Bridie

A variation of Bridget.
OTHER FORM: Bride.

Brittany

Taken from the name of a region of France, this is popular in the US.
OTHER FORMS: Britanee, Britani.

Brittney

A variation of Brittany.

Bronwen

From the Welsh, 'white breast', this is a very popular name in Wales.
OTHER FORM: Bronwyn.

Brooke

From the Old English, 'small stream'. It has become known through the American filmstar Brooke Shields.

Brooklyn

An elaboration of Brooke.
OTHER FORM: Brooklynne.

Brunhilde

From the Old German, 'armour' and 'fight'. One of the legendary Valkyries, depicted in Wagner's *Ring* cycle.
OTHER FORMS: Brunhild, Brunhilda, Hilda, Hilde.

Bryna

An Irish female form of Brian, meaning 'strength with virtue'.

Bryony

This is the name of a wild climbing plant and comes from the Greek, 'to grow luxuriantly'.

Buffy

A pet form of Elizabeth.

Bunty

A traditional name for a pet lamb, it is commonly used as a nickname.

B ~ Boys

Bailey
From the Middle English, 'the outer wall of a castle'.

Bala
From the Sanskrit, 'young child'.

Baldwin
From the Old German, 'bold friend'.
OTHER FORMS: Boden, Bowden.

Balthasar
From the Hebrew, 'God protect the king'. One of the Magi who brought gifts to the baby Jesus.
OTHER FORM: Belshazzer.

Bala
From the Sanskrit, 'young child'.

Baldie
A Scottish short form of Archibald.

Balu
Originally a short form of Balakrishna, where the first part of the name comes from the Sanskrit word, 'young'.

Baptist
From the Greek, 'to dip'. Baptism in the Christian church is when people are received into the Christian faith.
OTHER FORMS: Baptiste, Gianbattista.

Barclay
Scottish surname, now used as a first name.

Bardolf
From the Old German, 'bright' and 'wolf'.

Barnabas
From the Aramaic, 'son of exhortation'. The name of an unofficial Apostle in the Bible.

Barnaby
A variation of Barnabas.

Barney
A short form of Barnaby.

Barrett
A modern name from the surname.

Baron

From the Latin, 'man' or 'warrior' this name is given to a man with immense power.

OTHER FORM: Barron

Barry

From the Celtic, 'spear', this was the name of several early Irish Christians.

OTHER FORMS: Bairre, Bari, Barrie.

Bartholomew

From the Hebrew, 'son of Talmai'. Talmai was the surname of the Apostle Nathaniel. St Bartholomew's Hospital in London was founded in the 12th century and there was a fair of that name until the 19th century.

SHORT FORMS: Bart, Barty, Bat, Tolomey.

Bart

A short form of Barton or Bartholomew.

Barton

From the Old English, 'barley' and 'town'.

Basil

From the Greek, 'royal'. A 4th-century saint, with six other members of the same family being saints.

SHORT FORMS: Bas, Basie, Baz, Bazza.

Bastian

A short form of Sebastian.

OTHER FORM: Bastien.

Baxter

Old English for a baker, this was originally a surname.

Baudoin

The French version of Baldwin. It was the name of a king of Belgium.

Bayard

From the Latin, 'reddish-brown colour'.

Beau

From the French, 'handsome'. Known through Beau Brummell, the fashionable friend of King George IV.

Beaufort

From the French, 'handsome and strong'.

Beaumont

From the French, 'beautiful mountain'.

Bede

From the Middle English, 'prayer'. Known through the Venerable Bede, the first known writer of English prose.

Bellamy
From the French, 'handsome friend'.

Ben
A short form of Benjamin or Benedict.

Benedict
From the Latin, 'blessed'. St Benedict was the founder of the Benedictine Order. Shakespeare used the name in *Much Ado about Nothing*.
OTHER FORMS: Ben, Benedick, Bennet, Benny.

Benjamin
From the Hebrew, 'son of my right hand'. He was the favoured youngest son of Jacob, in the Bible.
Short forms: Ben, Bennie, Benjy.

Benjie
A short form of Benjamin.

Bennett
An old form of Benedict.

Benson
Originally meaning 'son of Ben', this is taken from the surname.

Bentley
Possibly from Old English, 'to become'.

Berg
From the German, 'mountain'.
OTHER FORMS: Borg, Borje, Bourke, Burk.

Berkeley
From the Old English, 'birch tree' and 'meadow'.
OTHER FORMS: Barcley, Berkl(e)y.

Bernard
From the German, 'brave as a bear'. There were two saints who bore the name.
SHORT FORMS: Barny, Bernhard.

Bernd
The German version of Bernard.
OTHER FORM: Berndt.

Bernie
A short form of Bernard.

Berry
From the name of the soft fruit. Also short for Bertram.

Bert
From the German, 'bright', this is short for a number of names, such as Albert, Herbert and Robert.
OTHER FORM: Burt.

Bertie
A variation of Bert.

Bertram

From the Old German, 'bright raven', the bird owned by the Norse god Odin.
OTHER FORMS: Bert, Bertie, Bertrand.

Bertrand

This French name means 'bright shield'.
SHORT FORMS: Bert, Bertie.

Beverly

From the Old English, 'beaver meadow', this name is given to both girls and boys.
OTHER FORM: Beverley.

Bevis

A French name meaning 'bow'.
OTHER FORMS: Bevan, Bevin.

Bharat

From the Sanskrit, 'being maintained'. India's official name after independence.

Bhaskar

From the Sanskrit, 'the sun'.
OTHER FORM: Bhaskara.

Bill

Short form of William

Björn

Scandinavian name for 'bear'. Popular because of the Swedish tennis player, Björn Borg.

Blaise

A French name meaning a person from Blois, or the Latin for 'stammerer'.
SHORT FORMS: Blase, Blaze

Blake

A surname used as a first name, from the Old English meaning 'black, dark-complexioned'.

Bond

Possibly Germanic meaning 'bound', this is a surname used as a first name.
OTHER FORMS: Bondie, Bondon, Bondy.

Booker

From the Old English, 'written document', also 'beech tree'. Ancient runes were written on tablets of beechwood.

Boone

From the Norse, 'blessing', or the Latin, 'good'.
OTHER FORMS: Bone, Boonie.

Booth

From the Norse, 'dwelling'. William Booth founded the Salvation Army.

Boris

From the Russian, 'fight'.

Boyd

From the Gaelic, 'yellow hair', it is the name of a Scottish clan.

OTHER FORMS: Bow, Bowen, Bowie.

Brad

A short form of Bradley, used as a given name in the US and Canada.

Bradley

From the Old English, 'wide meadow'.

SHORT FORM: Bradd.

Brady

From the Old English, 'to broaden' or from a Gaelic surname.

Brandon

A variation of Brendon.

Brendan

An Irish name meaning 'with stinking hair'. The 6th-century St Brendan was reputed to have sailed to discover America.

OTHER FORMS: Bran, Brandin, Brenden.

Brennan

A pet form of the Irish name Bren, probably meaning 'sorrow, tear'.

Brett

From the Old French, 'a Briton or Breton'. Popular in the US.

OTHER FORM: Bret.

Brewster

From the Old English, 'to brew, make ale'. More common in the US.

Brian

From the Celtic, 'strong'. Brian Boru was a famous Irish king in the 11th century.

OTHER FORMS: Briant, Brion, Bryant.

Brice

'Son of Rice', from the German, 'rich'. The name of a 5th-century French saint.

OTHER FORMS: Bryce, Bryson.

Brien

A variation of Brian.

Brigham

From the Old Italian, 'to fight'. More usual in the US.

Brock

From the Old English, 'badger', this is the name usually given to a badger in children's stories.

Broderic

Anglo-Saxon, 'from the broad ridge'.

Bronson

From the Old English, 'the son of the brown-haired man'.

Bruce

From the French, 'woods'. Robert the Bruce was King of the Scots in 1306 and won independence for Scotland.
OTHER FORMS: Brucey, Brucie.

Bruno

The German for 'brown' this is the traditional name for a bear.
OTHER FORMS: Bruin, Bruna.

Brutus

From the Latin, 'heavy, stupid'. Brutus was one of Julius Caesar's assassins.

Bryan

A variation of Brian.

Bryn

From the Welsh, 'hill'.
OTHER FORMS: Brin, Brynmor.

Buck

Usually used as a nickname, it was an 18th-century term for a dashing, fashionable man.

Buddy

Occasionally used as a first name, but more often as a nickname.
SHORT FORM: Bud

Burford

From the Old English, 'ford by the castle'.

Burgess

From the Latin, 'fortified place'. Formerly the name of an MP who represented a town or university.

Burhan

Arabic for 'evidence' or 'proof'.

Burl

From the Anglo-Saxon, 'cup-bearer'.

Butler

From the Old French, 'chief steward'. Taken from the surname connected with an old Irish family.

Buxton

Taken from a place name in Derbyshire.

Byron

From the Old English, 'stall, cow-shed'. Lord Byron was a romantic English poet.
OTHER FORMS: Biron, Byram, Byrom.

C ~ Girls

Caitlin
An Irish Gaelic form of Katherine, it is generally pronounced with the stress on the first syllable.

Caitrin
An Irish Gaelic form of Katherine.

Calandra
From the Greek, 'lark'.

Calantha
From the Greek, 'beautiful blossom'.
OTHER FORMS: Cal, Calanthe, Callie, Cally.

Calliope
From the Greek, 'beautiful-voiced'. The name of a musical instrument that used to be played on the Mississippi steamboats.

Callie
Originally a short form of Caroline, it is now used as a name in its own right.
OTHER FORMS: Cal, Cally, Kallie, Kally.

Cally
Probably a variation of Kelly, mainly found in the US. Also a short form of Caroline.
OTHER FORM: Callie.

Calypso
From the Greek, 'to conceal'. The name of a sea-nymph who kept Odysseus on her island for seven years.

Camellia
Flowering shrubs with beautiful, coloured flowers. *La Dame aux Camellias* was a beautiful courtesan in the story by Dumas.

Camilla
The name of a warrior queen, possibly meaning 'one who helps at sacrifices'.
OTHER FORMS: Camille, Milla, Millie, Milly.

Candace
An ancient title of the Queen of Ethiopia.
OTHER FORMS: Candice, Candis, Candy.

Candida

From the Latin, 'white'. The name of several saints it has only been used in Britain from the 10th century.

SHORT FORM: Candy.

Caprice

From the Latin, 'head' and 'hedgehog' this has come to mean a wayward, impulsive person.

Cara

The Italian for 'dear' and also from the Celtic, 'friend'.

OTHER FORMS: Kara, Karena.

Carina

From the Latin, 'beloved'.

Carissa

A variation of Charissa.

Carita

From the Latin, 'kindness', from which comes the word 'charity'.

Carla

The female form of Carl.

OTHER FORMS: Carlie, Karla.

Carlotta

The Italian form of Charlotte.

Carly

A pet form of Carla.

Carma

From the Sanskrit, 'destiny'.

OTHER FORM: Karma.

Carmel

From the Hebrew, 'garden', this is a mountain in Israel which Mary was reputed to visit with the infant Jesus.

OTHER FORMS: Carmela, Carmelina.

Carmelita

A diminutive of Carmel.

Carmen

From the Latin, 'to sing' this is the Spanish form of Carmel. Carmen is the heroine of the opera by Bizet.

OTHER FORMS: Carmina.

Carnation

The name of a flower, from the genus that includes sweet william.

Carol

From the Old French, 'to celebrate in song'.

OTHER FORMS: Carel, Carola, Karel.

Carole

The French form of Carol.

Caroline

This name comes from the Italian female form of Charles (Carlo).
OTHER FORMS: Carlyn, Caddy, Caro, Lyn.

Carolyn

A variation of Caroline.

Carrie

A short form of Caroline.

Caryl

A variation of Carol.

Carys

A modern Welsh name from the word meaning 'love'.

Cass

A short form of Cassandra.

Cassandra

From the Greek, 'entangler of men'. In Greek legend she was a princess of Troy who foretold the truth but was never believed.
SHORT FORMS: Cass, Cassie, Sandra.

Cassia

From the Greek, 'herb', this family of shrubs is prized for its fragrant scent and healing properties.
OTHER FORMS: Caswell, Kezia(h).

Cassidy

An Irish surname, this is used as a first name in the US.
SHORT FORM: Cass.

Cassie

A pet form of Cass.

Cate

A short form of Catherine. Best known for the filmstar Cate Blanchett.

Cath

A short form of Catherine.

Catharine

An English version of Catherine.

Catherine

From the Greek, 'pure'. The name of two saints and of the wife of Henri II of France, it was originally spelt with a 'K'.
SHORT FORMS: Catie, Catlin, Trinny.

Cathleen

This is the Irish form of Catherine.

Cathy

A short form of Catherine.

Catrin

The Welsh form of Katherine and a short form of Catriona.

Catriona

A Gaelic form of Katherine, it is the title of a book by Robert Louis Stevenson.
OTHER FORMS: Catrin, Catrina, Katrina, Riona.

Cayleigh

A variation of Kayleigh.

Cecile

A French form of Cecily.

Cecilia

An Italian martyr who was the patron saint of music.
SHORT FORMS: Cecil, Cecily, Cicily, Ciss, Cissy.

Ceinwen

From the Welsh, 'lovely' and 'blessed' or 'white'.

Celandine

From the name of the yellow flower.

Celeste

From the Latin, 'heavenly', this is no longer an exclusively French name.
OTHER FORM: Celesta.

Celestine

Mainly French variation of Celeste.
OTHER FORM: Celestina.

Celia

Originally a short form of Cecilia, but now a name in its own right.

Celina

A variation of Selina.
OTHER FORM: Céline.

Ceri

A popular Welsh name, from the Welsh for 'love'.
OTHER FORMS: Cari, Carys, Cerian, Cerys.

Ceridwen

The name of a Celtic goddess who was the mother of the poet, Taliesin. It is pronounced with a hard 'c'.

Cerise

From the French, 'cherry' or the name of the pinkish-red colour.

Cerys

A variation of Ceri

Chandra

From the Sanskrit, 'the moon'. Although the moon is a god in the Hindu religion, this is a girl's name.

Chandrakala

From the Sanskrit, 'moonbeams'.

Chanel

The name of a famous French perfume named after the fashion designer 'Coco' Chanel.

OTHER FORMS: Shanell, Shannel.

Chantal

From the French, 'to sing' this name came from the surname of a 16th-century saint.

OTHER FORM: Chantalle.

Chantel

A variation of Chantal.

OTHER FORMS: Chantelle, Shantelle.

Charis

From the Greek, 'grace', the 'Ch' is pronounced 'K'.

OTHER FORMS: Chrissa, Karis.

Charissa

Probably a combination of Charis and Clarissa.

Charity

From the Latin, 'brotherly love'. One of the three great Christian virtues, with Faith and Hope.

OTHER FORMS: Carita, Charista, Charry, Cherry.

Charleen

A variation of Charlene.

Charlene

A female form of Charles.

OTHER FORMS: Charline, Sharlene.

Charlie

A pet form of Charlotte, used as a given name in the US.

Charlotte

French female form of Charles. Princess Charlotte was the daughter of George IV.

SHORT FORMS: Charlie, Chattie, Lottie, Sharlott, Totty.

Charmaine

This name is probably a form of Charmian.

OTHER FORM: Sharmaine.

Charmian

From the Greek, 'drop of joy'. Shakespeare used the name in *Anthony and Cleopatra*.

SHORT FORM: Carmen.

Charulata

An Indian name meaning 'beautiful'.

Chastity

From the Latin, 'pure, virtuous'.

Chelsea

The name of a fashionable area in London, this is popular due to Chelsea Clinton, the US President's daughter.
OTHER FORMS: Chelsi, Chelsie.

Chelsey

A variation of Chelsea.

Cher

A short form of Cheryl or from the French, 'dear'. Well known because of the American singer of the same name.

Cherene

Mainly used in the US, an elaboration of Cher.

Cherida

A modern name, associated with the Spanish word for 'darling'.

Cherie

The French for 'dearest' this is the name of the wife of the British Prime Minister, Tony Blair.
OTHER FORMS: Cher, Sheree, Sherrie, Sherry.

Cherise

From the French for cherry.

Cherish

From the word meaning 'to care for', this is a modern invention.

Cherry

A pet form of Charity. Charles Dickens used the name in *Martin Chuzzlewit*.

Cheryl

Probably another form of Cherry.
OTHER FORMS: Cher, Cheralyn, Cherelle, Cherilyn, Sheryl.

Cheryth

A combination of Cher and Gwyneth. Cherith is also the name of a place in the Bible.

Chevvone

A variant of Sheena or Siobhan.

Cheyenne

This is the name of a famous American Indian tribe. It is pronounced 'Shyann'.

Chintana

An Indian name which means 'meditation'.
OTHER FORM: Chintanika.

Chloe

From the Greek, 'green, verdant'. The name of the goddess of young crops, in poetry it is often given to country girls.
OTHER FORMS: Clea, Cloe.

Chloris

From the Greek, 'blooming', this was the name of the goddess of flowers.
OTHER FORMS: Chlorine, Cloris.

Chris

A short form of Christable and Christine.

Chrissie

A short form of Christine, also used in its own right.

Christa

A short form of Christine.

Christable

A compound of 'Christ' and the Latin 'bella'.
SHORT FORMS: Chris, Chrissy, Christie.

Christelle

A variation of Crystal.

Christene

A variation of Christine.
OTHER FORM: Christeen.

Christian

This name is used for both sexes and originally denoted someone of the Christian faith.
SHORT FORMS: Chris, Chrissie.

Christiana

A variation of Christina.

Christie

A pet form of Christine.

Christin

A variation of Christine.
OTHER FORMS: Kristen, Kristin.

Christina

A variation of Christine.

Christine

The female form of Christian, which means 'a follower of Christ'.
OTHER FORMS: Crysten, Krista, Kristin.

Chrysanthemum

From the Greek, 'gold flower'. The autumn-flowering plants originally come from China.
OTHER FORM: Chryseis.

Ciara

An Irish name, meaning 'dark-haired'.
OTHER FORM: Kiara.

Cicely
Another form of Cecilia.

Cilla
A short form of Priscilla.

Cinderella
From the French, 'ashes'. The fairy-tale girl who becomes a princess.
SHORT FORMS: Cindy, Ella.

Cindy
A short form of names such as Cynthia and Lucinda.
OTHER FORMS: Cin, Cinie, Sindy.

Clare
From the Latin, 'clear, bright'. St Clare of Assisi founded the order of Poor Clares in the 13th century.
OTHER FORMS: Claribel, Clarrie.

Claire
A variation of Clare.

Clarice
A variation of Clarissa.

Clarina
Another form of Clare.

Clarinda
A variation of Clare.

Clarissa
From the Latin, 'most famous'. The name of the heroine of an 18th-century novel.
OTHER FORMS: Clara, Clarice, Clarrie.

Claudette
The French female form of Claud.

Claudia
The female form of Claud, a Roman name brought to England in the 1st century.
OTHER FORMS: Claude, Clodia.

Claudine
The French short form of Claude.

Clemency
From the Latin, 'mildness'. The Roman goddess of pity.
OTHER FORMS: Clem, Clemmie.

Clementina
From the Latin, 'merciful'.
OTHER FORMS: Clementine, Tina.

Cleopatra
From the Greek, 'glory of her father'. She was a queen of Egypt famous for her beauty and sexual allure.
SHORT FORMS: Cleo, Cleta.

Clio

From the Greek, 'to praise'. She was one of the nine muses in mythology.

Cliona

A beautiful Irish legendary fairy-woman.
OTHER FORMS: Clidna, Cliodhna.

Clodagh

This is the name of an Irish river, which only started to be used as a first name in the 20th century.
OTHER FORM: Claudia.

Clotilda

From the Old German, 'loud battle'. She was a French queen who converted her husband to Christianity.

Clover

A flower name. The four-leaved clover is supposed to bring good luck.
SHORT FORM: Clova.

Colette

A French female form of Nicola. The French author of the same name wrote the novel, *Gigi*.
OTHER FORMS: Colet, Collette, Kalotte.

Colleen

This is the Irish for 'girl' and is widely used in Australia and the US.

Comfort

From the Latin, 'to give solace' this name was used by the Puritans.

Conception

From the Latin, 'conceive', it usually refers to the Virgin Mary.
OTHER FORMS: Concepcion, Concha.

Conchita

A mainly Spanish name and a short form of Concepcion.

Connie

A short form of Constance.

Constance

The Latin for 'constancy', this was a name popular with the Puritans
OTHER FORMS: Constancy, Constantina.

Consuela

From the Latin, 'to free from sadness', this is a Puritan name.
OTHER FORMS: Consolata, Consuelo.

Cora

A short form of Corinna.
OTHER FORM: Kora.

Coral

From the Latin, 'from the sea'.
OTHER FORM: Coralie.

Cordelia

From the Celtic, 'daughter of the sea'. Shakespeare used the name for one of King Lear's daughters.

OTHER FORMS: Cordie, Cordula, Delia, Della.

Cornelia

The female form of Cornelius.

SHORT FORMS: Cornie, Corny, Neila, Nellie, Nell.

Corinna

From the Greek, 'the maiden'. The name was used by Herrick in his poems.

OTHER FORMS: Corin, Corinne.

Corisande

This name was used in medieval romances and was given to the mistress of King Henri II of France.

Cosima

From the Greek, 'universe, harmony'.

Cressida

From the Greek, 'the golden one'. Chaucer wrote about her and Shakespeare used the name in *Troilus and Cressida*.

SHORT FORM: Cressy.

Crystal

From the Greek, 'ice', this is the name of a clear quartz used for jewellery.

OTHER FORMS: Christel, Krystal.

Crystin

A short form of Christine.

Cushla

An Irish term of endearment, 'beat of my heart'.

Cybele

The mythical mother goddess of Anatolia, who watched over fertility.

OTHER FORMS: Cybela, Cybill.

Cynthia

Another name for Artemis or Diana, the Greek goddess, it means 'of Mount Cynthos'.

SHORT FORMS: Cimmie, Cindie, Cindy, Cynth.

C ~ Boys

Cadfael
Welsh for 'battle metal'. A popular character in the British television series.

Cadmus
The mythical founder of Thebes he invented the alphabet and married the daughter of Aphrodite.

Cadoc
The name of a 6th-century Welsh saint.

Cadogan
From the Welsh, 'battle honour'.

Cadwallader
From the Welsh, 'battle chief', the name has been found in Wales since the 7th century.

Caesar
Julius Caesar, the conqueror of Britain, was a famous Roman emperor.
OTHER FORMS: Casar, Cesar, Cesare.

Cahan
The Irish form of Kane.

Caius
A Roman name meaning 'rejoice'.
OTHER FORMS: Cai, Gaius, Kai, Kay.

Cale
Found mainly in the US, this is either taken from the surname or a short form of Caleb.

Caleb
From the Hebrew, 'dog' or 'imperial', this name is fashionable in the US.
SHORT FORMS: Cale, Kale.

Callum
From the Latin, 'dove'. This is a typically Scottish name from which comes Malcolm.
SHORT FORMS: Calum, Colm, Colum.

Calvin
From the Latin, 'bald', this derives from the French surname, Chauvin.
SHORT FORMS: Caiv, Cal, Vin, Vinny.

Camden
From the Gaelic, 'winding valley'.

Cameron

From the Gaelic, 'crooked nose'. It is the name of a Scots clan and can also be used for girls.

Campbell

From the Latin, 'beautiful field', this is the surname of a famous Scots clan.
SHORT FORMS: Cam, Camp, Campie.

Canute

A variation of Knute, the name of the king who tried to hold back the waves.

Caradoc

From the Welsh, 'beloved'. In the form Caractacus, it was the name of an ancient Briton who fought the Romans in the 1st century.

Carey

A variation of Cary.

Carl

A German form of Charles.

Carlo

The Italian form of Charles.
OTHER FORMS: Carlos.

Carlton

From an old English place name, meaning 'countryman's farm'.

Carol

Derived from the Latin, Carolus, this is a central European name. The name of a former king of Rumania.
OTHER FORMS: Cahal, Cathal.

Cary

Famous because of the film star, Cary Grant.

Casey

From the Celtic, 'brave in battle'.
OTHER FORM: Caswell.

Casimir

From the Polish, 'announcement of peace'. He is the patron saint of Poland.
OTHER FORMS: Casey, Cass, Cassy, Kazimir.

Caspar

From the German, 'imperial'. This was the name of one of the Wise Men who brought gifts to the baby Jesus.
OTHER FORMS: Casper, Cass, Jasper, Kaspar.

Cassidy

Possibly from the Welsh, 'trickster'.
OTHER FORMS: Cass, Cassie, Cassy.

Cassius

A Roman, he was one of the conspirators who plotted to kill Julius Caesar.
OTHER FORMS: Case, Cash, Casius, Cazzy.

Cathal

From the Celtic, 'battle' and 'rule', this is the name of an Irish saint in the 7th century.

Caxton

Taken from the surname, known for the William Caxton who started the first printing press in England.

Ceallach

A traditional Irish name, with the meaning 'bright-headed'.

Cecil

From the Latin, 'blind'. It is the surname of an famous English family.
OTHER FORMS: Ceci, Ces, Cis, Sissy.

Cedric

From the Celtic, 'model of generosity'. It is the name of a character in Sir Walter Scott's novel *Ivanhoe* and also of the boy in *Little Lord Fauntleroy*.
SHORT FORMS: Cad, Cerdic, Rick, Ricky.

Chad

The name of a 7th-century saint who was Bishop of Lichfield. Also the name of the founder of the Samaritans.

Chance

From the Anglo-Norman for 'good fortune'. Used mainly in the US.

Chandler

From the French for candle.
OTHER FORMS: Chan, Chaney, Cheney.

Chander

From the Sanskrit, 'the moon', this is the masculine equivalent of Chandra.

Chandrakant

From the Sanskrit, 'loved by the moon', it refers to a jewel formed by the moon's rays, in classical Hindu texts.

Chapman

From the Old English, 'trade'.
OTHER FORMS: Chap, Chappy, Mannie.

Charles

From the Old German, 'man'. The name of many kings it is now borne by the heir apparent to the English throne.
OTHER FORMS: Chae, Charlie, Chas, Chuck.

Charlton

Another form of Carlton.

Chase

A surname used as a first name, particularly in the US. A character in the television series *Falcon Crest*.

Chester

From the Latin, 'fort', this is the name of an English city.

Chet

A Thai word meaning 'brother'.

Chetan

An Indian name meaning 'awareness'.

Chip

A short form of Christopher.

Chris

A short form of Christopher.

Christian

From the Greek, 'anointed one', the word means a person who believes in Jesus Christ. The name of the hero of *Pilgrim's Progress*.
SHORT FORMS: Chris, Christie, Kit, Kris, Kristian.

Christie

A short form of Christopher, used in its own right.

Christopher

From the Greek, 'bearing Christ'. St Christopher is the patron saint of travellers.
SHORT FORMS: Chip, Chris, Kester, Kit.

Chuck

Originally a nickname, from an English term of endearment.

Clarence

The name means 'of Clare'. The Duke of Clarence took the title from the town of Clare in Suffolk in the 14th century.
OTHER FORMS: Clancy, Claron, Sinclair.

Clark

The name meant someone who could read and write. The film star Clark Gable made the name popular.
OTHER FORM: Clarke.

Claud

From the Latin, 'crippled'. The Emperor Claudius was lame but became a great ruler.
OTHER FORMS: Claude, Claudian, Claudie.

Claus

This is the German form of Nicholas.

Clay

From the Old English meaning a fine-grained earth.

OTHER FORMS: Cle, Cletis, Cletus, Klay.

Clayton

A longer version of Clay.

OTHER FORM: Klayton.

Clemence

From the Latin, 'mildness'.

SHORT FORMS: Clem, Clemmie.

Clement

From the Latin, 'merciful', it was the name of an early saint and of several popes.

OTHER FORMS: Clemente, Clim, Klement, Klimt.

Clifford

The name of several places in Britain, this surname is now used as a first name.

SHORT FORM: Cliff.

Clifton

This name means, 'settlement by the cliff'.

Clint

A short form of Clinton, made famous by the actor Clint Eastwood.

Clinton

From the Middle English, 'hilltop town', this is more usually a surname. Used as a first name in the US.

Clive

From the Old English, 'steep, high rockface'. Robert Clive (Clive of India) made the name popular in the 18th century.

Clyde

From the Welsh, 'heard from far away', this is the name of a Scottish river.

OTHER FORMS: Cly, Clydell.

Clywd

A variation of Clyde.

Cobb

A short form of Jacob.

Cody

An Irish surname meaning 'descendant of a helpful person'. It was the surname of Buffalo Bill, the hero of the Wild West.

OTHER FORMS: Codey, Kody.

Colby

Originally the name came from a farm owned by a Norseman called 'Koli.

Cole

From the Middle English, 'coal'.
OTHER FORMS: Colby, Colin, Colton, Colyer.

Coleman

Anglo-Saxon for 'follower of the doves' or Middle English for 'coal-miner'.
OTHER FORMS: Col, Cole, Colman.

Colin

A French form of Nicholas. Also from the Gaelic, 'puppy' or 'youth'.
SHORT FORMS: Col, Cole, Collin.

Colm

The Irish form of Columba.

Colton

A variation of Colby.

Colwyn

From the Welsh, 'hazel grower'.

Comhghall

From the Gaelic, 'fellow hostage'. The 6th-century St Comhghall founded the monastery at Bangor.

Con

A short form of Conrad or Connor, used in its own right.

Conal

An Irish name from the Celtic, 'high and mighty'.

Conan

From the Old Irish, 'lover of hounds'. The name of one of the great kings in Ireland.
OTHER FORMS: Con, Connor, Conny.

Conn

From the Gaelic, 'chief', and also a short form of Connor.

Connor

From the Gaelic name meaning 'lover of hounds'.
SHORT FORMS: Con, Conny.

Conrad

From the Old German, 'bold counsel'.
SHORT FORMS: Con, Curt, Kurt.

Corbin

From the Old French, 'raven'. Made popular by the actor Corbin Bernsen.

Corey

This name originated as an Irish surname and is popular in the US.
OTHER FORMS: Cory, Korey, Kory.

Corin

From the name of an ancient Roman god.. It is used in poetry for a love-sick shepherd.

Cormac

From the Greek, 'tree trunk'. A popular name in Ireland.

OTHER FORM: Cormick.

Cornelius

From the Latin, 'a horn', this was the name of a 3rd-century saint who was also a pope.

OTHER FORMS: Conney, Corney, Cornie.

Cosmo

From the Greek, 'order' this is the name of two saints and was used by the Italian Medici family in the form 'Cosimo'.

Courtney

This probably comes from a French place name, but is possibly from the French, 'short nose'. Also used as a girl's name.

Craig

From the Gaelic, 'rock', this was taken from a Scottish surname.

Crawford

From the Old English, 'crow'.

SHORT FORMS: Craw, Crow.

Crispian

The name of St Crispin's brother, who was also a saint.

Crispin

From a surname meaning 'curly-headed'. The name of a 3rd-century saint.

Cromwell

From the Welsh, 'winding stream'. The Puritan, Oliver Cromwell, ruled England as Lord Protector in the 17th century.

Crosby

From the Middle English, 'cross'.

Curran

From the Old English, 'to churn, agitate'.

OTHER FORMS: Curr, Currey, Currie.

Currie

A variation of Curran.

Curtis

From the French, 'courteous', it is more usual in the US.

Cuthbert

From the Old English, 'famous, bright'. It was the name of a 7th-century saint, the Bishop of Lindisfarne.

OTHER FORMS: Cudbert, Cuddy.

Cy

A short form of Cyrus.

Cynan

From the Welsh, 'chief' or 'outstanding'.
OTHER FORMS: Cynin, Cynon, Cynyr.

Cyprian

From the Latin, 'native of Cyprus'. He was a 3rd-century bishop of Carthage.

Cyril

From the Greek, 'lord'. The name was borne by several early saints and St Cyril devised the Russian Cyrillic alphabet.
SHORT FORM: Cy.

Cyrus

A Greek form of the Persian, 'sun' or 'throne'. This was the name of the founder of the Persian Empire in the 6th century BC and of various saints.
SHORT FORMS: Cy, Cyro.

D ~ Girls

Daffy
A short form of Daffodil and Daphne.

Daffodil
A flower name from the Dutch for asphodel.
SHORT FORMS: Daf, Daffy.

Dalia
A modern version of Dahlia.

Dahlia
From the name of the flower, called after Anders Dahl, a Swedish botanist.
OTHER FORM: Daliah.

Daisy
From the Old English, 'day's eye', a flower name which is sometimes a nickname for Marguerite, the French word for daisy.

Dakota
The name of an American Indian tribe, this is used in the US.

Dale
Originally the name for someone who lived in a dale or valley.
OTHER FORMS: Dael, Daile.

Damara
A variation of Damaris.

Damaris
Possibly from the Greek, 'calf'. The name of a woman in the Bible who was converted to Christianity by St Paul.

Dana
From the Old English for a Dane. The name of a pagan Irish fertility goddess.
OTHER FORMS: Dane.

Daniella
A variation of Danielle.

Danielle
The French female form of Daniel.
OTHER FORMS: Daniela, Danette, Danny.

Daphne

From the Greek, 'bay tree, laurel'. The name of a nymph who was turned into a laurel to get away from the god Apollo.
SHORT FORMS: Daf, Daffy.

Daralis

From the Old English, 'beloved'.

Darcie

From the French, 'from the fortress'.

Darcy

The name of a family who came from Arcy in France. The surname of the hero of Jane Austen's *Pride and Predjudice*.
OTHER FORM: Darcey.

Daria

The female form of Darius.

Darlene

A modern name from the endearment 'darling'.

Davida

Female form of David.
OTHER FORMS: Davita, Vida, Vita.

Davina

From the Hebrew, 'beloved'.
OTHER FORM: Davinia.

Dawn

This may have been the translation of aurore, meaning dawn in French. Aurora was the Greek goddess of the dawn.

Dayna

A variation of Dana.

Deanna

A variation of Diana.
OTHER FORM: Deanne.

Dearbhail

An old Irish name meaning 'daughter of Fal (poetic name for Ireland)'.

Deb

A short form of Deborah.

Debbie

A variation of Deb.

Deborah

From the Hebrew, 'bee', it is a biblical name and was used by Puritans in the 17th century.
SHORT FORMS: Debbi, Debra, Debs.

Dee

Usually a nickname for someone whose name begins with the letter 'D'.

Deepika

From the Sanskrit, 'little lamp' it is one of the names for Kama, god of love.

Deirbhile

An old Irish name from the Gaelic, 'daughter of the poet'. It was the name of a 6th-century saint.

Deirdre

A tragic heroine in Celtic legend, known as 'Deirdre of the Sorrows'.
OTHER FORM: Deidra.

Delfine

From the Greek, 'dolphin'.
OTHER FORM: Delfina.

Delia

From Delos, the birthplace of the Greek goddess Artemis and popular with poets in the 17th and 18th centuries. Best known for the cookery writer Delia Smith.

Delicia

From the Latin, 'to give pleasure'.
OTHER FORMS: Delight, Delizia.

Delilah

A biblical character who cut off Samson's hair, the source of his strength, and betrayed him to the Philistines.
OTHER FORM: Delila.

Della

Possibly a short form of Adela, used in its own right.

Delma

From the Spanish, 'from the sea'.

Delphine

Associated with the flower, delphinium, this was the name of a 4th-century saint, St Delphinus of Bordeaux.

Delta

From the name of the Greek letter 'D'.

Demelza

A modern name derived from a place in Cornwall. It was made popular by the television series *Poldark*.

Demetria

The Greek goddess of fertility and an earth mother.

Dena

Female form of Dean, from the Anglo-Saxon, 'glen'.

Denise

Female form of Denis.

Denna

A variation of Dena.

Dervila

A variation of Dervla.

Dervla

The Anglicized form of an old Irish name meaning 'daughter of the poet'. Best known for the travel writer, Dervla Murphy.

Desdemona

From the Greek, 'woman of bad fortune'. The virtuous wife of Othello in Shakespeare's play.
OTHER FORM: Desmona.

Desirée

From the Latin, 'desired', this name was given by the French to a long-awaited child.
OTHER FORM: Desideria.

Destiny

From the word for fate, this name is popular in the US.
OTHER FORMS: Destinie, Destiney.

Deva

From the Sanskrit, 'god, divine'. Hindu name for the goddess of the moon.
OTHER FORM: Devaki.

Devin

A variation of Devon.

Devon

From the name of the English county, this is usually pronounced with the stress on the first syllable by parents in the US.
OTHER FORMS: Davon, Devonne.

Dextra

The female form of the Latin 'right-handed', implying skill with the hands.

Dhanishta

From the Sanskrit, 'star'.

Di

A short form of Diana.

Diamanta

From the Greek, 'unconquerable'.

Diamond

Mainly known in the US. There is a vogue for using the names of precious stones.

Diana

The mythological goddess of the moon and hunting. This name has become popular due to Diana, Princess of Wales.
OTHER FORMS: Di, Didi, Dyanne.

Dianne

A variation of Diana.

Diandrea
A modern blend of Diana and Andrea.
OTHER FORM: Diandra.

Diantha
From the Greek, 'heavenly flower'.
OTHER FORM: Dianthe.

Didi
A short form of Diana.

Dido
The mythical founder of Carthage, and lover of Aeneas.

Dilys
From the Welsh, 'perfect, true'.
SHORT FORM: Dilly.

Dinah
From the Hebrew, 'judgement', this was the name of one of Jacob's daughters in the Bible.
SHORT FORM: Dina.

Dione
The name of a mythical Greek character, meaning 'divine queen'.

Dionne
From the Greek, 'god'. A popular name among Afro-Americans.

Diva
From the Latin, 'goddess', this is the epithet for famous opera singers or other star performers.

Divya
From the Sanskrit, 'divine lustre'.

Dodie
A short form of Dorothy.

Dodo
A short form of Dorothy.

Dolly
A pet name for Dorothy or Dolores.
OTHER FORM: Doll.

Dolores
From the Spanish, 'Mary of the Sorrows'.
OTHER FORMS: Delores, Deloris, Lola, Lolita.

Dominique
The female form of Dominic.
OTHER FORM: Dominica.

Donalda
A female form of Donald.

Donata
From the Latin, 'gift'.
OTHER FORM: Donita.

Donna

From the Italian, 'lady', used in the US during the 20th century. It is also a short form of Madonna.

OTHER FORMS: Donni, Donny.

Donella

A female form of Donald.

Dora

A short form of Theodora or Dorothy.

OTHER FORM: Dorrie.

Dorcas

From the Greek, 'gazelle', it is an interpretation of the Aramaic, Tabitha. It was used by women who made clothes for the needy.

Doreen

From the Irish name, Dorean.

OTHER FORMS: Dorren, Dorrie, Dorinne.

Doria

From Oscar Wilde's novel *The Picture of Dorian Gray*.

OTHER FORMS: Doriana, Dorianne.

Dorinda

A poetic version of Dora.

Doris

From the Greek, 'Dorian woman'. A mythical goddess of the sea, she was the mother of the Nereids or sea-nymphs.

OTHER FORMS: Dorrie, Dorris.

Dorothea

From the Greek, 'gift of God'. It was the name of two minor saints.

SHORT FORMS: Dora, Thea.

Dorothy

The English version of Dorothea. The abbreviation 'Doll' or 'Dolly' became the name of a toy baby.

SHORT FORMS: Dodo, Dodie, Dot, Dottie.

Dorrie

A short form of Doris.

Dorrity

The Scottish form of Dorothy.

Dove

The symbol of peace and gentleness.

OTHER FORM: Dova.

Dreda

A short form of the rare Etheldreda.

Drew

A female version of the short form of Andrew.

Drusilla

A female form of the Latin Drusus, possibly meaning 'firm'. A biblical name, it was used by the Puritans.

SHORT FORMS: Drusie, Drusy.

Dulcie

From the Latin, 'sweet', known from the actress, Dulcie Gray.

OTHER FORMS: Dulcibella, Dowsabel.

Durga

From the Sanskrit, 'inaccessible', it is the name of a Hindu goddess, the wife of Shiva.

Dusha

From the Russian, 'soul'.

Dusty

Female form of Dustin, known from the singer Dusty Springfield.

Dymphna

From the Irish, 'fawn' it is the name of a Flemish saint. There is a Belgian hospital bearing her name.

OTHER FORMS: Devnet, Dympna.

Dysis

From the Greek, 'sunset'.

D ~ Boys

Dafydd
The Welsh form of David.

Dag
A pet form of David.

Dai
A short form of Daffyd.

Daithi
From the Hebrew, 'nimbleness'.

Dale
Taken from the surname this is used mainly in the US..

Daley
From the Irish surname, meaning 'assembly' or 'gathering'.

Dallas
From the Gaelic, 'meadow stance'. This is used as a first name mainly in the US.

Daly
A variation of Daley.

Damian
From the Greek, 'tamer'. Four saints bore this name.

Damien
A variation of Damian.

Damon
From the Greek, 'fate'. The mythological characters, Damon and Pythias were so devoted that they offered to die for each other.

Dan
Short form of Daniel.

Dandy
A short form of Andrew.

Dane
Meaning 'man from Denmark', or a variation of Dean.
OTHER FORM: Dana.

Daniel

From the Hebrew, 'God has judged'. The name of the biblical prophet whose faith protected him when he was thrown to the lions.

OTHER FORMS: Deiniol, Domhnall.

Danny

A pet form of Dan.

Dante

From the Italian, 'to endure'. The name of the author of *The Divine Comedy* and of the Pre-Raphaelite painter, Dante Gabriel Rossetti.

Darcy

An Irish surname meaning 'descendant of the dark one'. See also the female form.

Darell

A US variation of Darrell.

Daren

A variation of Darren.

Darius

A 6th-century Persian king. The name means 'protector'.

Darien

A variation of Dorian.

OTHER FORM: Darian.

Darrell

From the French name of a village meaning 'courtyard'.

OTHER FORMS: Darryll.

Darren

A popular mid-20th century name of unknown origin.

OTHER FORM: Darran.

Darryl

A variation of Darrell.

Darshan

From the Sanskrit, 'to see', this name is supposed to give spiritual benefit to the onlooker.

Darwin

From the Old English, 'lover of the sea'. Charles Darwin wrote the controversial *Origin of Species*.

Dave

A short form of David, used in its own right.

David

The Hebrew for 'beloved'. As a young man he killed the giant Goliath and became the second king of Judah.

SHORT FORMS: Dai, Davie, Davey.

Davis
Taken from the surname and used mainly in the US.

Davy
A pet form of Dave.

Dean
From the Old English, 'valley'. The name was made popular by the American film actor, Dean Martin.
OTHER FORMS: Dene, Denn, Dino.

DeAndre
A popular name with Afro-American families in the late 20th century.

Declan
The name of an early Irish saint connected with Ardmore.

Deepak
From the Sanskrit, 'little lamp', it is used for the Hindu god of love.
OTHER FORM: Dipak.

Deiniol
An ancient Welsh name, of possible Celtic origin.

Del
A pet form of Derek.
OTHER FORM: Dell.

Delbert
A 20th-century name formed from Delroy or Delmar and Albert.

Delmar
From the Latin, 'of the sea'.
OTHER FORMS: Delmer, Delmor(e).

Delroy
From the Latin, 'of the king'.
SHORT FORMS: Del, Roy.

DeMarco
Popular with Afro-Americans.
OTHER FORMS: DeMarcus, DeMario.

Demetrius
From Demeter, the Greek 'earth mother' goddess. Dimitri or Dmitri are variations which are found in Russia.
OTHER FORMS: Demetrios, Demitrus.

Den
A short form of Denis or Dennis.

Dene
A variation of Dean.

Denholm
This is the name of a place meaning 'island valley'.
OTHER FORM: Denham.

Denis

This is the French form of Dionysius, the Greek god of wine and revelry. It is the name of the patron saint of France.

SHORT FORMS: Den, Denny.

Denzil

From Denzell, this is an old Cornish place name.

Dennis

A variation of Denis.

Denny

A short form of Dennis.

Denzil

A Cornish name meaning 'high stronghold'.

Derek

From the Old German, 'ruler of the people'.

SHORT FORMS: Derry, Dirk, Ricky, Rik.

Dermot

From the Irish name Diarmid, 'free from envy'. He was a legendary figure who eloped with the queen of Tara and was killed for it.

Derrick

A variation of Derek.

Derry

A pet form of Derek.

Derwent

From the Celtic, 'clear water'. This is the name of several rivers in Britain.

Des

A short form of Desmond.

Desmond

From the Irish surname meaning, 'man from Munster'.

SHORT FORMS: Desi, Desy, Dezi.

Dev

From the Sanskrit, 'god'. The term Deva is used for royalty and priests.

OTHER FORMS: Deb, Deo.

Devdan

From the Sanskrit, 'gift of the gods'.

OTHER FORMS: Debdan, Deodan.

Devin

From the Celtic, 'poet'.

Devon

Also used as a girl's name, this is probably from the English county of the same name. Known because of the cricketer Devon Malcolm.

Dewi

A Welsh form of David. The 5th-century St Dewi became the first bishop of Menevia, now known as St Davids.

Dexter

Possibly from the Latin, 'right-handed'. The original name was female, meaning 'dyer'.

SHORT FORMS: Dex, Dexy.

Dezi

A short form of Desmond.

Diarmaid

The Irish form of Dermot.

OTHER FORM: Diarmait

Diarmid

A variation of Diarmaid.

Dick

A short form of Richard.

OTHER FORMS: Dickie, Dicky.

Dickon

An old short form of Richard.

Didier

The French male equivalent of Desirée.

SHORT FORM: Didi.

Diego

The Spanish form of James. The 15th-century saint of this name worked with the poor in the Canary Islands.

Digby

From the French, 'to dig a ditch or dike'.

Dilip

This is the name of many kings in the Hindu epics.

OTHER FORM: Duleep.

Dillon

From the Gaelic, 'faithful'.

OTHER FORM: Dylan.

Dimitri

A short form of Demetrius.

Dinsdale

A surname used as a first name, it means 'settlement surrounded by a moat'.

Dirk

The Dutch form of Derek. Best known through the actor Dirk Bogarde.

Dolph

A short form of Adolph.

Dolphus

A short form of Adolphus.

Dominic

From the Latin, 'of the Lord'. St Dominic founded the religious order of the Dominicans in the 13th century.

SHORT FORM: Dom.

Don

A short form of Donald and a variation of Donn.

Donal

From the Celtic, 'world' and 'rule'. This is an old Irish name.

OTHER FORM: Donall.

Donald

From the Celtic, 'proud ruler'. It was the name of a number of Irish and Scottish kings.

SHORT FORMS: Don, Donny.

Donn

An old Gaelic name meaning 'brown' or 'king'.

Donnan

The name of an Irish saint who founded a monastic community on the island of Eigg.

Donnel

From the Gaelic, 'hill-fort'.

OTHER FORM: Donnell.

Donnelly

A variation of Donnel.

Donovan

From the Irish for 'dark brown'. The singer with the same name made it popular in the 1960s.

Dorian

From the ancient Greek Dorians. Oscar Wilde appears to have introduced the name in his famous novel.

Dorrien

A variation of Dorian.

Dory

From the French, 'golden-haired'.

Doug

A short form of Douglas.

OTHER FORM: Dougie.

Dougal

From the Celtic, 'dark stranger', a name given to the Danish Vikings.

SHORT FORMS: Doug, Dug, Dugald, Duggy.

Douglas

From the Celtic, 'black stream'. This is the name of a powerful Scottish family.

SHORT FORMS: Dougie, Duggie.

Dove

From the Old English, signifying peace.
OTHER FORMS: Dovey, Duff.

Doyle

From the Irish, 'assembly', the name of
the Irish parliament.

Drake

From the Greek, 'serpent'. A variation of
dragon.

Drew

From the Old German, 'to carry'. A
variation of Andrew and Drogo.

Drogo

From the German, 'to carry'.
OTHER FORMS: Drago, Drewe, Dru.

Duald

An Irish name, probably from the
Gaelic, 'black-haired'.

Duane

An Irish surname, which probably means
'black'. The pop star Eddie Duane made
the name known in the 1950s.
OTHER FORMS: DeWayne, Du'aine.

Dudley

A place name and the name of the Earl
of Leicester, who was a favourite of
Queen Elizabeth I.
SHORT FORM: Dud.

Duff

A Scottish name from the Gaelic,
'black'.

Dugal

A variation of Dougal.

Duggie

A short form of Douglas.

Duke

From the Latin, 'leader'. A popular
nickname, especially in the world of
entertainment, it is also short for
Marmaduke.

Duncan

From the Gaelic, 'dark-skinned warrior'
it is the name of two Scottish kings.
OTHER FORMS: Donnchadh, Dunn, Dunc,
Dunkie.

Dunstan

From the Old English, 'greyish-brown', it
was the name of an English saint.
SHORT FORMS: Dunn, Dunst, Dustin,
Dusty.

Dustin

Popular in the US this is the name of the actor, Dustin Hoffman. It may derive from the Norse name, Thurstan.

Dwayne

A variation of Duane.

Dwight

From the Old English, 'white, fair'. Dwight D. Eisenhower made the name popular in the US.

SHORT FORMS: Diot, Doyt, Wit, Wittie.

Dylan

From the Welsh, 'the sea'. The name of the Welsh poet, Dylan Thomas and later of the singer, Bob Dylan.

E ~ Girls

Earla
A female form of Earl.

Earnestine
A variation of Ernestine.

Eartha
From the Old English, 'earth'. Best known for the singer, Eartha Kitt.
OTHER FORMS: Ertha, Erthel.

Ebony
The name of the black wood, this name has been popular with Afro-Americans. The song *Ebony and Ivory* by Paul McCartney and Stevie Wonder added to its popularity.
OTHER FORMS: Ebboney, Ebonie, Ebonnee.

Echo
The name of a nymph who pined away for love of Narcissus, until nothing was left but her voice.

Edana
A female form of the Irish name Edan, from the Gaelic, 'fiery'.

Eden
This name probably comes from the Garden of Eden in the Bible and can also be used for boys.

Edina
A variation of Edna.

Edith
From the Old English, 'fortunate war'. The name of two English saints in the 10th century.
SHORT FORMS: Edi, Edie.

Editha
A variation of Edith.

Edna
From the Old English, 'happiness' or the Hebrew, 'rejuvenation'.
OTHER FORMS: Adina, Edana, Edina.

Edwina
From the Old English, 'fortunate friend', this is the female form of Edwin.

Effie
Short form of Euphemia.

Eglantine
The name of a flower, alternatively 'sweet-briar', it was used by Chaucer.

Eileen
An Irish form of Evelyn.
OTHER FORMS: Aileen, Elly

Eiluned
From the Welsh, 'idol'.
SHORT FORMS: Linet, Luned, Lynette, Lynn.

Eilis
An Irish form of Elizabeth or of Alice.
OTHER FORMS: Eillish, Ailish.

Eirlys
From the Welsh, 'snowdrop'.

Eithne
Apparently this comes from the Gaelic, 'kernel' is a term of praise in old poetry. The name of various saints and queens.
OTHER FORMS: Aithne, Enya, Ethna, Ethne.

Ekata
From the Sanskrit, 'unity'.

Elaine
From the French name, Hélène, or from the Welsh 'fawn'. Elaine fell in love with Lancelot in the Arthurian legends.
SHORT FORM: Elain.

Elana
From the Hebrew, 'oak tree'.

Electra
From the Greek, 'amber'. The mythological Electra killed her mother and her mother's lover.
OTHER FORM: Elektra.

Eleri
An old Welsh name of unknown origin.

Elfrida
Female form of Alfred.

Eliane
A French form of Elaine.

Elinor
A variation of Eleanor.

Elisabeth
A variation of Elizabeth. The 's' form is used in the Bible and in continental Europe.
SHORT FORMS: Elisa, Lisa.

Elissa

Short form of Elizabeth.
OTHER FORM: Elise.

Eliza

Short form of Elizabeth.

Elizabeth

From the Hebrew, 'oath of God'. The 'z' spelling is more usual in England and became popular from Queen Elizabeth I.
OTHER FORMS: Bess, Beth, Betty, Eliza, Libby, Lizzy.

Elke

A German form of Alice.

Ella

From the Old English, 'fairy maiden' or the Old German, 'all'.
OTHER FORMS: Ala, Ela.

Ellen

An old English form of Helen.
SHORT FORM: Nell.

Ellie

A short form of Eleanor.

Elma

The Turkish for 'apple'.

Eloise

From the French name Heloise, the tragic lover of Abelard. Both names can be spelt with an umlaut on the first 'e' (Elöise).
OTHER FORM: Eloisa.

Elora

From the Greek, 'light'.

Elsa

A short form of Elizabeth. Elsa is the heroine of Wagner's opera *Lohengrin*.

Elsie

A Scottish short form of Elspeth.

Elspeth

Scottish abbreviation of Elizabeth.

Elspie

A pet form of Elspeth.

Eluned

From the Welsh, 'idol', derived from the old Welsh name Luned or Lunet.

Elvira

A Spanish name introduced to England by the Visigoths. The name of a character in Noel Coward's *Blythe Spirit*.
OTHER FORMS: Elva, Elvia.

Emer

A Celtic name for a legendary heroine, with many talents and much beauty.
OTHER FORM: Eimhir.

Emerald

A short form of Esmeralda and also from the green-coloured precious stone.

Emilia

The Italian form of Emily, also used in the English-speaking world.

Emily

From the Roman family name, Aemilius. The name of the 19th-century novelist Emily Brontë.
OTHER FORMS: Em, Emmy, Milly.

Emma

From the Old German, 'universal'. The name of the queen who married two English kings in the 11th century and of the heroine of Jane Austen's novel.
OTHER FORMS: Emmie, Emmy.

Emmeline

A variation of Emily.

Ena

From the Old Irish, 'fire'. The name of an English princess who became Queen of Spain and of a character in the television series *Coronation Street*.

Enfys

A modern name from the Welsh for 'rainbow'.

Enid

From the Welsh, 'life, soul', the name was used by Tennyson in his poetry.

Enora

From the Greek, 'light'.

Eolanda

From the Greek, 'dawn', this is a variation of Yolanda.

Erica

The botanical name for heather.
OTHER FORM: Erika.

Erin

A poetical name for Ireland.
OTHER FORM: Errin.

Erma

From the German, 'army maid'.

Ermyntrude

An old-fashioned name, for which the short form is Emma.

Erna

A female short form of Ernest.

Ernestine

The female form of Ernest.

Esmée

The French for 'esteemed', this name is more usually Aimée in France.
OTHER FORMS: Esma, Esmé.

Esmeralda

Spanish for 'emerald', the name was used by Victor Hugo for the heroine of *The Hunchback of Notre Dame*.

Essylt

A variation of Isolda

Estella

A variation of Estelle.

Estelle

From the French, 'star'. Heroine of Dickens' *Great Expectations*.
OTHER FORMS: Esther, Stella.

Esther

A biblical name from the Hebrew, 'myrtle', it was used by the Puritans.
OTHER FORMS: Essie, Ester, Hester.

Etain

A traditional Irish Gaelic name, maybe from a Celtic sun goddess.
OTHER FORMS: Eadan, Etan.

Ethel

From the Anglo-Saxon, 'noble', it is the short form of Etheldreda and Ethelinda.

Ethna

A variation of Eithne.
OTHER FORM: Ethne.

Etta

A short form of Henrietta
OTHER FORM: Ettie.

Eufemia

A variation of Euphemia.

Eugenie

From the Greek, 'well-born'. The name of the empress married to Napoleon.
OTHER FORM: Eugenia.

Eulalia

From the Greek, 'sweetly spoken'. This was the name of a 4th-century Spanish saint.

OTHER FORMS: Eula, Eulalie.

Eunice

From the Greek, 'happy victory', this is a biblical name and was used by the Puritans.

OTHER FORM: Unice.

Euphemia

From the Greek, 'well-spoken'. A name mostly found in Scotland.

SHORT FORMS: Effie, Eppie, Phemie.

Eustacia

The female form of Eustace.

Eva

The Latin form of Eve.

Evadne

From the Greek, 'fortunate'. Known through the first name of one of the characters in the television series *Hinge and Bracket*.

Evangeline

From the Greek, 'bringer of good news', it is the title of a poem by Longfellow.

OTHER FORM: Evangelina.

Evania

From the Greek, 'tranquil'.

Eve

In the Bible this is the name of the first woman created by God and comes from the Hebrew, 'life'.

OTHER FORMS: Evie, Evita.

Evelyn

From the Old German, 'hazel nut'. The Irish form is Eibhlin and the Norman form was Aveline.

OTHER FORMS: Eveline, Evelyne.

Evita

A diminutive of Eve. Best known through the wife of the Argentinian dictator General Peron, whose story was made into a musical.

Evonne

A variation of Yvonne.

E ~ Boys

Eachan
From the Gaelic, 'little horse'. Also the Irish form of Hector.

Eamon
Irish for Edmond. Eamon de Valera was President of Ireland from 1959-73 and Eamon Andrews was a popular television presenter.

Eamonn
A variation of Eamon.

Earl
From the Old English, 'nobleman' or 'chief'.
OTHER FORM: Erle.

Earnest
Variation of Ernest used more in the US.

Ebenezer
From the Hebrew, 'stone of help'. In the Bible, Samuel set up a memorial stone to commemorate the Israelites' victory over the Philistines. The name of the miser in Dickens' *A Christmas Carol*.

Ed
A short form of Edgar, Edmund or Edward.

Edan
The Irish and Scottish form of Aidan. It was the name of an Irish saint.

Eddie
A pet form of Ed.

Eden
Probably taken from the biblical Garden of Eden. Mainly used in the US.

Edgar
From the Old English, 'lucky spear'. King Edgar was King Alfred's grandson and the first real king of England. The name of a character in *King Lear*, Shakespeare's play.
SHORT FORMS: Ed, Eddie.

Edison
Taken from the surname, meaning 'son of Ed'. Mainly known in the US.

Edmund

From the Old English, 'happy protection'. It was the name of two saints and two English kings.

SHORT FORMS: Ed, Eddie, Ted, Teddy.

Edsel

From the Anglo-Saxon, ' profound thinker'.

Edward

From the Old English, 'fortunate guardian'. The name of many English kings from Edward the Confessor onwards.

SHORT FORMS: Ed, Eddie, Ned, Neddy, Ted, Teddy.

Edwin

From the Old English, 'happy friend'. St Edwin was the first Christian king of Northumbria.

OTHER FORMS: Ed, Eduin, Edwyn.

Egan

English form of the Gaelic name, Aogan.

Egbert

From the Old English, 'shining sword'. The name of a 7th-century saint and of the first king of a united England.

Egon

From the Old English, 'strong' or 'formidable'.

Eldon

Taken from a place name, this is mainly used in the US.

Elgar

From the Old English, 'noble spear'. Edward Elgar was an English composer who wrote the famous *Land of Hope and Glory*.

OTHER FORMS: Algar, Alger, Elger.

Eli

From the Hebrew, 'height'. In the Bible he was the high priest who brought up the prophet Samuel.

Elias

The Greek form of Elijah.

OTHER FORMS: Ellis, Eliot, Elliot.

Elihu

A variation of Eli.

Elijah

From the Hebrew, 'the Lord is my God'. He was one of the early prophets in the Bible.

Eliot

A variation of Elliot.

OTHER FORM: Elliott.

Elisha

From the Hebrew, 'God is my help'. In the Bible he was the prophet who succeeded Elijah.

OTHER FORMS: Elias, Elizur, Elkan, Ely.

Ellard

From the Old German, 'alder tree'.

OTHER FORMS: Ellary, Elston, Ellwood.

Ellis

A variation of Elias.

Elmer

From the Old English, 'famous' and 'noble'. The surname of two American brothers who were leaders in the American Revolution.

OTHER FORMS: Aylmer, Edmer, Elman.

Elmo

A variation of Elmer.

Elroy

From the Spanish, 'the king'. Leroy is the French form.

Elston

From the Old English, 'noble' and 'town'.

OTHER FORMS: Elsdon, Elton.

Elton

A variation of Elston. The name is associated with the singer, Elton John.

Elvin

From the Old English, 'elf-like'.

OTHER FORMS: El, Elva, Elwin, Elwyn.

Elvis

A variation of Elvin, the name was popularised by the singer, Elvis Presley.

Emanuel

A variation of Emmanuel.

Emil

The German for 'industrious'.

Emlyn

A Welsh name, which may be derived from the Latin, Aemilius.

Emmanuel

From the Hebrew, 'God is with us'. In the Bible it is the name given to the Messiah by the prophet Isaiah.

OTHER FORMS: Manuel, Manny.

Emmet
Anglo-Saxon for 'the industrious ant'.

Emrys
The Welsh form of Ambrose.

Enoch
From the Hebrew, 'dedicated'. He was the son of Cain and father of Methuselah in the Bible.

Enos
From the Hebrew, 'man'. In the Bible he was the son of Seth.

Eoan
A variation of Eugene.

Eoghan
From the Gaelic, 'born of yew', this is the Gaelic for the Irish county, Tyrone.

Eoin
The Gaelic form of John.

Ephraim
From the Hebrew, 'fruitful', this was a biblical name that was used by the Puritans.
SHORT FORM: Eph.

Erasmus
From the Greek, 'loved, desired'. St Erasmus or Elmo is the patron saint of sailors. It was the name of a Dutch scholar in the 16-17th century.
SHORT FORMS: Ras, Rasmus.

Eric
A popular Scandinavian name, it was brought to Britain by the Danes about the 9th century.
OTHER FORMS: Rick, Rickie, Ticky.

Erin
From the Gaelic, 'peace', this is a poetic name for Ireland.

Erle
A variation of Earl.

Ern
A short form of Ernest.

Ernest
From the Old German, 'serious business', it was brought to Britain by the Hanoverians. Made popular by Oscar Wilde's play *The Importance of Being Earnest*.
OTHER FORMS: Earnest, Ern, Ernie.

Ernesto
The Italian form of Ernest.

Ernie
A pet form of Ern.

Ernan
An Irish name, possibly from the Gaelic, 'iron'.

Ernst
The German form of Ernest.

Errol
Possibly a German form of Earl. Errol Flynn was a romantic swashbuckling film star.
OTHER FORMS: Rollo, Rolly.

Erskine
A Scottish surname it was brought to prominence by the writer and politician Erskine Childers.

Erwin
A variation of Irwin.

Esmé
More often used as a girls's name sometimes with another 'e' at the end.

Esmond
From the Old English, 'guardian, protector', this is a name that is not often used in modern times.

Esmund
A variation of Esmond.

Ethan
From the Hebrew, 'firmness', it is used several times in the Bible.

Ethelbert
The old form of Albert.

Euan
A Scottish variation of Eugene.

Eugene
From the Greek, 'well-born', this was the name of four popes.
OTHER FORMS: Eoan, Ewan, Ewen, Gene.

Eusibius
From the Greek, 'pious'. The 3rd-century Eusibius was a noted historian.

Eustace
From the Greek, 'rich in corn', 'fruitful'. St Eustace was a 2nd-century Roman martyr.
SHORT FORMS: Stacie, Stacy.

Evan
This is a Welsh form of John.
OTHER FORMS: Iefan, Ieuan, Ifan.

Evander

The name of the legendary hero who founded the city in Italy on which Rome was built later.

Evelyn

This surname is used for boys, although the name is also used for girls with various spellings.

Everard

From the Old German, 'brave boar', the name was introduced to England by the Normans.

OTHER FORMS: Everett, Ewart.

Ewan

Scottish form of John or of the Irish Eoghan.

Ewart

From the Old French, 'ewer, jug'.

Ewen

A variation of Ewan.

Ezekiel

From the Hebrew, 'may God strengthen'. It is the name of a prophet in the Bible.

Ezra

From the Hebrew, 'help'. The name of one of the prophets in the Bible and of the 20th-century poet, Ezra Pound.

F ~ Girls

Fabia
The female form of Fabius, from the old Roman family name, said to derive from 'bean'.

Fabienne
The French female form of Fabian.

Fabiola
St Fabiola was a 4th-century Roman saint who founded the first Western hospital, not only for the sick but also for healthy pilgrims.

Fae
A variation of Fay

Fahimah
From the Arabic, 'discerning', 'intelligent'.

Faith
From the Latin, 'trust, devotion'. One of the three major Christian virtues.
SHORT FORMS: Fae, Faye.

Fancy
From the Greek, 'to make visible', and so someone who has whims and wishes for dreams to come true.
OTHER FORM: Fancie.

Fanny
Previously a short form of Frances and Myfanwy, but now a name in its own right.

Fallon
The English form of the Irish surname 'O Fallamhain', or 'leader'. It became known through the character in the television series *Dynasty*.

Farah
From the Arabic, 'joy, cheerfulness'.
OTHER FORM: Farrah.

Farhanah
From the Arabic, 'delighted'.

Farida
From the Arabic, 'unique' or 'gem.

Fatima

From the Arabic, 'chaste', 'motherly'. It was the name of the Prophet Mohammed's daughter and is popular with Black Muslims. In the Christian world there are several shrines to Our Lady of Fatima.

Faustine

This name means fortunate in Italian and Spanish.
OTHER FORMS: Fausta, Faustina.

Fawn

From the French, 'young deer'.

Fay

From the French, 'fairy', this is a short form of Faith and of Euphemia.

Fedora

A short form of Theodora.

Felice

The French form of Felicia.

Felicia

A female form of Felix, it was the name of a Roman goddess of good fortune.

Felicity

From the Latin, 'happiness', it was the name of several early saints.
SHORT FORMS: Flick, Flicky, Flis.

Fenella

From the Gaelic, 'white-shouldered'.
OTHER FORMS: Fionola, Fionnuala.

Fern

From the plant name.

Fernanda

A female form of Ferdinand.

Ffion

From the Welsh for foxglove flower, it is a poetic word used for the cheek of a beautiful girl.

Fi

A short form of Fiona.

Fidelma

A variant of the traditional Irish name, Feidhelm, which was borne by the legendary daughter of a beautiful female warrior.

Fifi

A pet name for Josephine.

Filipa
A variation of Phillipa.

Filma
From the Old English, 'misty veil'.

Filomena
From the Greek, 'loving harmony'.
OTHER FORM: Philomena.

Finch
A bird name occasionally used as a first name.

Finola
A variation of Fionuala.

Fiona
From the Gaelic, 'fair, white'.
SHORT FORM: Fi.

Fionnuala
In Irish legend Fionnuala was turned into a swan and wandered the lakes and rivers until Christianity came to Ireland.
SHORT FORM: Nuala.

Flair
A derivative of the French, 'discerning', this is a modern name.

Flavia
From the Latin, 'golden yellow'. This was the name of several early saints.

Fleur
From the French, 'flower', the name was used by Galsworthy in *The Forsyte Saga*.

Fleurette
A diminutive of Fleur.

Flis
A short form of Felicity.

Flicky
A short form of Felicity.
OTHER FORM: Flick.

Flo
A short form of Florence.

Flora
From the Latin, 'flower'. She was the Roman goddess of flowers and the spring. Flora Macdonald helped Bonnie Prince Charlie to escape from Scotland.
OTHER FORMS: Flo, Florrie.

Florella
A diminutive of Flora.

Florence

From the Latin, 'flourishing'. Florence Nightingale was named after the town in Italy and was the founder of modern nursing.

SHORT FORMS: Florrie, Flos, Flo, Floy.

Florrie

A short form of Flora and Florence.

Flossie

A short form of Florence.

Flower

A variation of Fleur, this is used as a term of endearment.

Floy

A short form of Florence.

Fortuna

From the Latin, 'luck'. Fortuna was the Roman goddess of good luck and of fertility.

OTHER FORM: Fortunata.

Fran

A short form of Frances.

OTHER FORM: Franny.

France

A short form of Frances, or in honour of the country.

Francene

A variation of Francine.

Frances

The female form of Francis.

SHORT FORMS: Fran, Franny.

Francesca

This is the Italian form of Frances. Francesca di Rimini was a legendary beauty in the 13th century.

SHORT FORMS: Francie, Frankie.

Francine

A diminutive of Françoise.

Françoise

The French form of Frances.

Frankie

A short form of Frances or Francesca. Best known from *The Ballad of Frankie and Johnny*.

Franny

A short form of Frances.

Frea

A variation of Freya.

Freda

A short form of Elfreda or Winifred.

Frederica

From the Old German, 'peaceful ruler'.
SMALL FORMS: Freida, Frida.

Frederique

The French form of Frederica.

Freya

From the Norse, 'noble lady', she was the
Norse goddess of love and beauty.
OTHER FORM: Freyja.

Frida

A short form of Frederica.

Frieda

A short form of Frederica.

Fulvia

The female form of the Roman family
name, Fulvius. Fulvia was the wife of
Mark Antony.

F ~ Boys

Fabian
From the Latin family name Fabianus. St Fabianus was pope in the 3rd century and the Fabian Society took its name from the Roman general Fabius, who was known as the 'delayer'.
OTHER FORMS: Fabio, Fabius.

Fabien
A French variation of Fabian.

Fadil
From the Arabic, 'virtuous' or 'distinguished'.

Fairfax
This was the nickname for someone with long, fair hair. It is the surname of a distinguished English family.

Faisal
A variation of Faysal.

Falcon
A name taken from the bird of the hawk family

Falkner
From the Greek, 'falcon', the birds used for hunting.
OTHER FORMS: Faulkner, Fowler.

Farley
From the Old French, 'fair' and the Middle English, 'meadow'.
OTHER FORMS: Fair, Fairleigh, Farly.

Farquhar
A Scottish name from the Gaelic, 'man' and 'friendly'.

Farr
Taken from the surname, this possibly means 'a traveller'.

Farrell
A variation of Fergal, with the Gaelic meaning 'valorous man'.
OTHER FORM: Farrall.

Fawaz
From the Arabic, 'victorious'.

Fayad
From the Arabic, 'generous'.

Faysal
The Arabic name means someone who is a judge. It is the name of kings of Iraq and Saudi Arabia.

Feargus
A variation of Fergus.

Feisal
A variation of Faysal.

Felix
From the Latin, 'happy' or 'lucky', it is the name of many early saints. Also the name for a cat.

Fenn
From the Old English, 'marsh', this first name is mainly known in the US.

Ferdie
A short form of Ferdinand.

Ferdinand
From the Latin, 'wild, bold'. The name of kings of Castile, one of whom was a saint.
SHORT FORMS: Ferdi, Ferdie, Fern.

Fergal
From the Gaelic, 'valorous', it was the name of a murderous 8th-century king of Ireland.

Fergie
A short form of Fergus, used in its own right.

Fergus
From the Gaelic, 'man' and 'vigorous'.
OTHER FORMS: Feargus, Fergie.

Fidel
From the Latin, 'faithful'. The name of the Cuban dictator, Fidel Castro.

Fielding
From the Old English, 'field'.
SHORT FORMS: Fie, Field, Fielder.

Fife
A variation of Fyfe.

Fillan
From the Gaelic name meaning 'wolf'. St Fillan was a missionary in Scotland in medieval times.

Finbar
The Gaelic, 'fair-haired'. The name of at least three Irish saints.
OTHER FORMS: Fionnbharr, Bairre.

Findlay
A variation of Finlay.

Fingal
From the Gaelic, 'fair stranger', it was used for the Vikings. A legendary Scottish warrior, he gave his name to Fingal's Cave.

Finlay
From the Gaelic, 'fair-haired soldier'. Finn Mac Coul is a great Irish hero, who was chosen to lead the Fenians.
OTHER FORMS: Fin, Finley.

Finn
A short form of Finbar, meaning 'white, fair'. The Irish hero Finn MacCool appears in the old legends.

Finnian
From the Irish, 'fair'. The name of a 6th-century British saint.

Fintan
A variation of Finn.

Fitz
From the Old English, 'son'. Traditionally added to the surname of a child born outside wedlock.

Flann
Originally an Irish nickname meaning 'red'.
OTHER FORM: Flannan.

Fleming
From the surname which derived from 'a man from Flanders'.

Fletcher
A surname meaning, 'maker of arrows'. It was the name of Fletcher Christian the leader of the mutiny on the *Bounty* in 1789.

Flint
The name of a hard rock, chosen for someone who shows strength and determination.

Flip
A short form of Philip.

Florent
The French male form of Flora.

Florian
The name of one of a pair of Greek twin saints.
OTHER FORMS: Fiorentino, Flory.

Floyd
A variation of Lloyd.

Forbes

From the Greek, 'fodder', this name is popular in Scotland.

Ford

From the Old English, 'shallow river-crossing', more common in the US where Henry Ford produced the model T Fords at the beginning of the 20th century.

Forester

From the surname for a woodsman.

Forrest

Originally a surname, from the German, 'guardian of the forest'.
OTHER FORMS: Forest, Forester, Foster.

Fortune

From the French, 'the lucky one'.
OTHER FORMS: Fortunato, Fortunio.

Foster

A variation of Forester.

France

A short form of Francis, or from the name of the country.

Francis

From the Latin, 'Frenchman'. St Francis of Assisi is the patron saint of the poor and the sick who founded the Franciscan Order of monks.
SHORT FORMS: Fran, Frank, Frankie.

Frank

A short form of Francis.

Franklin

From Middle English, 'free'. The first name of the American President Roosevelt.
SHORT FORMS: Frank, Frankie.

Fraser

Possibly derived form the French, 'charcoal maker'. The surname of a leading Scottish family.
OTHER FORM: Frasier.

Frazer

A variation of Fraser.

Fred

A short form of Frederick.

Freddie

A pet form of Fred.
OTHER FORM: Freddy.

Frederic

The French form of Frederick.

Frederick

From the Old German, 'peaceful ruler'. There have been several kings with this name.

OTHER FORMS: Frederik, Freddie, Freddy.

Freeman

Taken from the surname, meaning someone who was no longer a slave.

Frey

The male form of Freya.

Fulk

From the German, 'people' or 'tribe', this old name is used by some aristocratic families.

OTHER FORM: Fulke.

Fulton

A Scottish surname. Robert Fulton was the American engineer who designed the first commercial steamboat.

Fyfe

A Scottish name meaning, 'man from Fife'.

G ~ Girls

Gabriela
A female form of Gabriel.

Gabrielle
The French female form of Gabriel.
OTHER FORMS: Gay, Gabriella, Gabby.

Gaby
A short form of Gabriella.

Gae
From the English word meaning 'cheerful'.
OTHER FORMS: Gay, Gaye.

Gaea
A variation of Gaia.

Gaenor
A Welsh form of Jennifer.

Gaia
The mythological Greek earth mother. This name is an important one for environmentalists or feminists.

Gail
A short form of Abigail, now also used in its own right.
OTHER FORMS: Gale, Gayle.

Gala
A short form of the Russian, Galina.

Gardenia
A flower name for a sweet-smelling bloom.

Garnet
From the Old French, 'pomegranite'. The fruit has a deep red colour and there is also a gemstone of the same name.

Gauri
From the Sanskrit, 'white', this was a name for the wife of the Hindu god, Shiva.

Gay
From the French, 'lively, joyful'. Currently an epithet for homosexuals, it has lost its popularity as a first name.
OTHER FORMS: Gae, Gaye.

Gayle
A variation of Gail.

Gaynor
A medieval form of Guinevere, the name of King Arthur's wife.

Geena
A variation of Gina.

Geeta
A variation of Gita.

Gemma
From the Latin, 'precious stone'. It is the name of a 19th-century Italian saint.
OTHER FORMS: Germaine, Jemma.

Geneva
Possibly a short form of Geneviève. The name of a city in Switzerland.

Geneviève
A French name derived from the German, 'womankind'. She is the patron saint of Paris.
OTHER FORMS: Genny, Genovera, Genoveva, Gina.

Georgene
A variation of Georgine.

Georgette
The French female diminutive for Georges.

Georgia
The female form of George. The name of a 5th-century saint, it became popular in England under the Hanoverians.

Georgiana
A variation of Georgia.

Georgie
A pet form of Georgia or Georgina.

Georgina
A Latin form of Georgia.

Georgine
The French form of Georgina.

Geraldine
This means 'one of the Fitzgeralds' and was invented for a 16th century poem.
SHORT FORMS: Gerry, Jerry.

Germaine
A female form of the French name, Germain. Best known for the feminist writer, Germaine Greer.

Gerry
A short form of Geraldine.

Gertrude

From the Old German, 'strong spear', it is the name of a Dutch saint.

SHORT FORMS: Gert, Gertie, Trudi, Trudy.

Ghislaine

From the Old French, 'pledge, hostage', it is pronounced with a hard 'g' and no 's'.

OTHER FORM: Ghislane.

Gigi

A French name, a diminutive of Gilberte. Gigi is the heroine of the novel by Colette, which was made into a film of the same name.

Gilberte

The French female form of Gilbert.

Gilda

From the Old English, 'to gloss over', it means to add a thin layer of gold leaf to an object.

Gillaine

A modern form of Gillian.

Gillian

An English form of the Latin, Juliana.

OTHER FORMS: Gill, Jill, Jillian, Jilly.

Gina

A short form of Georgina and Regina.

Ginette

A short form of Geneviève.

Ginger

Originally a nickname for someone with red hair, it was the name of the film star Ginger Rogers.

Gini

A short form of Virginia.

Ginny

A short form of Virginia.

Gisèle

The French form of Giselle.

Giselle

From the Old German, 'pledge' or 'hostage'. Best known as the name of a ballet.

OTHER FORM: Gisela.

Gita

From the Sanskrit, 'song', it is also a short form of Margarita.

OTHER FORM: Geeta.

Gitana

From the Spanish, 'gypsy'.

Giulia

A variation of Julia

Giuletta
The Italian version of Juliet.

Glad
A short form of Gladys.

Gladys
The English form of Gwladys, the Welsh for 'ruler'.
SHORT FORMS: Glad, Gladdie.

Glenn
From the Celtic, 'valley', this is one of the oldest recorded names.
OTHER FORMS: Glenna, Glenne.

Glenda
From the Welsh, 'holy and good'. Best known for the actress and politician, Glenda Jackson.

Glenice
A variation of Glenys.

Glenis
A variation of Glenys.

Glenna
A female form of Glen.

Glenys
From the Welsh, 'holy'.
OTHER FORMS: Glennis, Glennys.

Gloria
From the Latin, 'glory', 'fame'. The name of a character in Bernard Shaw's play *You Never Can Tell*.

Glory
A variation of Gloria.

Glynis
From the Welsh, 'little valley', it is related to Glen and Glyn.
OTHER FORM: Glinys.

Gobnat
An Irish Gaelic name. St Gobnat founded a monastery in Co. Cork.

Golda
From gold, the most precious metal. Best known for Golda Meir, who was Prime Minister of Israel from 1969-74.
OTHER FORMS: Goldie, Goldina.

Goldie
From the nickname for someone with blonde hair. Best known for the actress Goldie Hawn.

Govindi
From the Sanskrit, 'cow-finding'. A name associated with the Hindu god, Krishna.

Grace

From the Latin, 'the graceful one'. Grace Kelly, the American film star married Prince Rainier of Monaco and was killed in a car crash.

OTHER FORMS: Gracia, Graciela, Grazia.

Gracie

A pet form of Grace.

Grainne

The legendary Irish princess, bethrothed to Finn, who eloped with Dermot and killed herself after Finn brought about his death.

Grania

A variation of Grainne.

Granya

A Russian variation of Grania.

Greer

A Scottish surname, from the Greek, 'the watchful mother', it was first used as a first name by the actress, Greer Garson.

OTHER FORM: Grier.

Greta

A short form of Margaret or Margarita. The Swedish reclusive film star Greta Garbo made the name popular.

OTHER FORMS: Gretel, Gretchen.

Gretchen

The German pet form of Margaret or Margaretta.

Griselda

Possibly from the Old German, 'grey' and 'battle'. Best known from the character in Chaucer's *Canterbury Tales*

OTHER FORMS: Grizel, Zelda.

Gudrun

From the German, 'war' and 'rune'.

Guendolen

A variation of Gwendolyn.

Guenevere

From the Welsh, 'fair' and 'holy'. The name of King Arthur's wife who fell in love with Lancelot.

Guinevere

A variation of Guenevere.

Gulab

From the Sanskrit, 'rose'.

Gus

A short form of Augusta.

OTHER FORM: Gussie.

Gustava

From the Scandinavian 'staff of the gods'.

Gwen

The short form of several Welsh names such as Gwendolen, it is now a name in its own right.

Gwenda

From the Welsh, 'fair and good'.

Gwendolen

From the Welsh, 'white ring', probably refering to the legendary moon-goddess.
SHORT FORM: Gwen.

Gwendolyn

A variation of Gwendolen.

Gwenllian

Traditional Welsh name meaning 'fair, flaxen'.

Gwenyth

A variation of Gwyneth.

Gwladys

Welsh form of Gladys.

Gwynedd

This name is taken from a region of Wales, now a county.

Gwyneth

A variation of Gwynedd.
SHORT FORM: Gwyn.

Gypsy

From the word for a traveller or Romany, it derived from Egyptian, as the travellers were supposed to come from Egypt.

G ~ Boys

Gabby
A short form of Gabriel.

Gabriel
The name of the Archangel who told the Virgin Mary that she was to bear the infant Jesus.
SHORT FORMS: Gabby, Gay.

Gad
From the Hebrew, 'fortunate'. In the Bible Gad is one of the 12 sons of Joseph and an ancestor of one of the tribes of Israel.

Gael
Probably from the Welsh, 'wild', this is the name for the Gaelic-speaking people of Ireland, Scotland and the Isle of Man.

Gage
From the French, 'pledge'.

Gaius
A variation of Caius.

Galahad
From the Gaelic, 'hawk in battle'. Sir Galahad was the son of the legendary Lancelot and the only Knight of the Round Table to reach the Holy Grail.

Galal
A variation of Jalal.

Gale
From the Old French, 'gallant, brave'.
OTHER FORMS: Gael, Gaylor.

Galil
A variation of Jalal.

Gall
The Irish saint accompanied St Columba on his mission to Europe in the 7th century.

Ganesh
From the Sanskrit, 'lord of the hosts', this is the name of the Hindu god Shiva's son.

Gareth

From the Welsh, 'gentle'. The name was used by Tennyson in his poem *Gareth and Lynnette*.

SHORT FORMS: Garth, Gary, Garry.

Garfield

From the Old English, 'promontory'. Well known for the West Indian cricketer Garfield Sobers.

SHORT FORM: Gary.

Garland

A wreath of flowers and leaves. This name is also given to girls.

Garret

From the French, 'to observe', it is also another form of Gerard.

OTHER FORM: Garrett.

Garry

A variation of Gary.

Garth

A variation of Gareth.

Gary

From the Old German, 'spear' and a short form of Gareth and Garfield. The film star Gary Cooper took his name from the American town.

OTHER FORM: Garry.

Garvin

From the Old English, 'friend in battle'.

SHORT FORMS: Gar, Vin, Vinny.

Gaspar

From the Persian, 'master of the treasure'.

OTHER FORMS: Caspar, Jasper, Kaspar.

Gaspard

A variation of Gaspar.

Gaston

A French name, which came from Gascon, a native of Gascony.

Gawain

From the Welsh, 'hawk of the plain'. Sir Gawain was one of the legendary Knights of the Round Table.

OTHER FORM: Gawaine.

Gavin

An Anglicized form of Gawain, it is now known world-wide.

OTHER FORMS: Gav, Gaven.

Gaylord

From the French, 'happy man'.

Gene

A short form of Eugene.

Geoffrey

Possibly from the Old German meaning 'peace of God'.
SHORT FORMS: Geoff, Jeff.

Geordie

A variation of George. It is the nickname for someone who comes from the north-east of England.

George

From the Greek, 'farmer'. St George is the patron saint of England and in the legend rescued a fair maiden from a dragon. The name has been borne by six English kings.
OTHER FORMS: Geo, Georgie.

Georges

The French form of George.

Ger

A short form of Gerald and Gerard.

Geraint

A Welsh name from the Old English Gerontius, from the Greek, 'old'.

Gerald

From the Old German, 'spear rule'. The name is popular in Ireland due to the powerful Fitzgerald family of Kildare.
SHORT FORMS: Ger, Gerry, Jerry.

Gerard

From the Old German, 'spear' and 'brave'.
OTHER FORMS: Gerrard, Jerrard, Jed.

Gerry

A short form of Gerald.

Gervais

From the Old German, 'armour bearer'. St Gervase was a 1st-century martyr.
OTHER FORM: Jarvis.

Gervase

A variation of Gervais.

Gib

A short form of Gilbert.

Gideon

From the Hebrew, 'he who cuts down'. A biblical figure who vanquished the Midianites. The name was used by the Puritans.
Short form: Gid.

Gilbert

From the Old German, 'bright hostage', it is the name of a medieval saint.
Short forms: Gib, Gilly, Bert, Bertie.

Gilchrist

From the Gaelic, 'servant of Christ'.

Giles

From the Greek, 'goatskin'. The patron saint of beggars and cripples, there are many churches dedicated to him.
OTHER FORMS: Gil, Gyles.

Gilles

The French form of Giles.

Gillie

An English gypsy name meaning 'song'.

Gilmore

From the Old Norse, 'deep glen' and the Old English, 'tree root'.
OTHER FORMS: Gillie, Gillmore, Gilmour.

Gilroy

From the Greek, 'servant', and the French, 'king'.

Giovanni

The Italian form of John.

Glen

From the Gaelic for 'valley'.
OTHER FORMS: Glenn.

Glyn

A Welsh name meaning 'glen' or 'valley'.
OTHER FORM: Glynn.

Glyndwr

From the Welsh, 'water' and 'valley'. Owen Glyndwr was a famous Welsh patriot.

Gobind

A variation of Govind.

Goddard

From the Old English, 'good advice'.
OTHER FORMS: Godard, Godart, Gothart.

Godfrey

From the Old German, 'God's peace', it is often confused with Geoffrey. There was a Norman St Godfrey who was Bishop of Amiens.

Godric

From the Old English, 'good ruler'. St Godric was a prosperous merchant who became a hermit to atone for his evil ways.
OTHER FORMS: Godrich, Goodrich.

Godwin

From the Old English, 'god' and 'friend'.

Golding

From the Old English, 'son of the golden one'.

Gomer

From the Hebrew, 'complete'. In the Bible this was the name of the grandson of Noah.

Goodwin

From the Old English, 'good friend'.

Gopal

From the Sanskrit, 'cow-protector' this name was applied to Krishna in medieval times.

OTHER FORM: Gopalkrishna.

Gordon

From the Old English, 'marsh' and the Scottish, 'wooded dell'. The surname of the British general who was killed at Khartoum.

SHORT FORMS: Gore, Gordy.

Gordy

A short form of Gordon.

Goronwy

A Welsh name of uncertain origin, borne by the legendary Lord of Penilyn.

Govind

A similar name to Gopal, with the same Sanskrit meaning.

Gowan

From the Old Norse, 'golden'. This is the Scottish name for small white or yellow flowers, especially the daisy.

OTHER FORM: Gowall.

Gower

A Welsh name from the name of the Welsh district.

Grady

From the Latin, 'degree, position'.

Graeme

A variation of Graham.

Grafton

Originally a local English place name, it was known in the US through the third Duke of Grafton.

Graham

The name of a Scottish clan, which is used as a first name.

OTHER FORMS: Graeme, Grahame.

Granger

From the Latin, 'grain', denoting a person who works on a farm.

Grant

The name of a famous Scottish clan and of the 18th President of the United States.

Granville

From the French, 'large town'.
OTHER FORM: Grenville.

Gray

An Old English name meaning 'grey'.
OTHER FORMS: Graydon, Grey, Greson.

Greeley

From the Old English, 'green meadow'.

Greg

A short form of Gregory.
OTHER FORM: Gregg.

Gregor

The Scottish form of Gregory.

Gregorio

The Italian form of Gregory.

Gregory

From the Greek, 'watchman'. St Gregory
was the pope who sent St Augustine to
England.
OTHER FORMS: Greg, Gregor, Gregour.

Grenville

A variation of Granville.

Greville

The Greville family were earls of
Warwick . Queen Elizabeth I granted
Warwick Castle to them.

Griffin

A variation of Griffith.

Griffith

From the Welsh, 'strong warrior', it has
always been a popular name in Wales.
SHORT FORM: Griff.

Grove

From the Old English, 'small thicket of
trees'.
OTHER FORM: Grover.

Gruffud

A Welsh form of Griffith.

Gruffydd

A Welsh form of Griffith.

Gustav

From the Old Norse, 'Gauer's staff', this
was the name of several Swedish kings.
Gustav Mahler was a well-known
Austrian composer.
OTHER FORM: Gustave.

Guthrie
From the Celtic, 'war hero'.

Guy
The original Norman names were Guido and Wido. Guy Fawkes was the conspirator who plotted to blow up the Houses of Parliament and is now commemorated on Bonfire Night, the fifth of November.

Gwill
A Welsh form of William.

Gwilym
A Welsh form of William.

Gwyn
From the Welsh, 'blessed' or 'white'.
OTHER FORMS: Gwynne, Wyn, Wynne.

Gwynedd
Taken from a Welsh place name.

Gwynfor
From the Welsh, 'blessed'and 'large'.

Gyles
A variation of Giles.

H ~ Girls

Habiba
From the Arabic, 'lover'.

Halcyon
From the Greek, 'kingfisher'.

Haley
A variation of Hayley.

Hana
From the Arabic, 'bliss, happiness' and the Japanese, 'flower'.

Hanna
A variation of Hannah.

Hannah
From the Hebrew, 'God has favoured me'. A biblical name, which was borne by the mother of the Prophet Samuel.

Happy
From the Old Norse, 'chance, good luck'.

Harmony
From the Greek, 'concord'.

Harriet
A female form of Harry, which has the French form, Harriette.
SHORT FORMS: Hattie, Hatty.

Harsha
From the Sanskrit, 'happiness'.

Hattie
A short form of Harriet.
OTHER FORMS: Hatty.

Hayley
From the surname meaning 'hayfield'. Best known for the actress Hayley Mills.
OTHER FORMS: Haley, Haylie.

Hazel
From the Old English, 'hazel-nut'.
OTHER FORMS: Hazelle.

Heath
Another name for Heather, which can be used for boys as well.

Heather

A flower name particularly popular in Scotland, where there are moors covered in the plant.

Heaven

From the Old English, 'abode of God'.

Hebe

From the Greek, 'youth'. Daughter of Zeus, she was the goddess of youth.

Hedda

From the German, 'war'. Best known for the heroine of Ibsen's play, *Hedda Gabler*.

Heena

A variation of Hina.

Heidi

A German form of Hilde, this name became popular due to the children's book *Heidi*.

Helen

From the Greek, 'the bright one'. St Helena was the British mother of Constantine the Great. Helen of Troy was a legendary beauty whose face could 'launch a thousand ships'.
OTHER FORMS: Elena, Ellen, Lena, Nell.

Helianthe

From the Greek, 'bright flower'.

Helga

From the Norse, 'holy'.

Helice

From the Greek, 'spiral'.

Heloise

A variation of Eloise.
OTHER FORM: Heloïse.

Hema

From the Sanskrit, 'golden'.

Henrietta

The female form of Henry.
SHORT FORMS: Etta, Ettie, Hetty.

Hephzibah

From the Hebrew, 'my delight is in her'. In the Bible she was the wife of the King of Judah.
OTHER FORMS: Hephziba, Hepzibah.

Hermia

A variation of Hermione.

Hermione

A female form of Hermes, the Greek messenger of the gods. Shakespeare uses the name in *A Winter's Tale*.

Hermosa
From the Spanish, 'beautiful.

Hero
In Greek myths she was the beautiful priestess of Venus.

Hespera
From the Greek, 'evening star'.
OTHER FORMS: Hesper, Hesperia.

Hester
A variation of Esther.

Hetty
A short form of Esther and Henrietta.

Hilary
From the Latin, 'lively, cheerful'.
OTHER FORMS: Hilaria, Hillary.

Hilda
From the Old English, 'battle'. There was an Anglo-Saxon St Hilda.
OTHER FORM: Hildie.

Hilde
The German form of Hilda.

Hillary
A variation of Hilary.

Hina
The Hindu name meaning 'henna', the red-coloured dye used for hair and fingernails.
OTHER FORMS: Heena, Henna.

Holly
From the Old English, 'holly tree'.
OTHER FORMS: Holli, Hollye.

Honey
From the sweet liquid produced by bees from nectar.

Honor
From the Latin, 'honour'.
OTHER FORMS: Honour.

Honoria
From the Latin, 'reputation, honour'.
OTHER FORMS: Anora, Honora, Nora.

Hope
From the Old English, 'to wish with optimism'. This is one of the three great Christian virtues.

Horatia
From the Latin, 'keeper of the house'. This is the female form of Horatio.

Hortense

From the Latin, 'garden'.
OTHER FORMS: Hortensia, Ortense, Ortensia.

Hoshi

From the Japanese, 'star'.

Hulda

The name of a prophetess in the Bible.

Humayra

The name given to his wife by the Prophet Muhammad.

Hyacinth

From the Greek, 'precious blue stone'. According to legend a purple flower sprang from the blood of the youth Hyacanthus.
OTHER FORMS: Cinthie, Giacinta, Jacinthe, Jackie.

H ~ Boys

Habib
From the Arabic, 'beloved'.

Hadley
From the Anglo-Saxon, 'heather' and 'meadow'.

Hadrian
The Roman emperor Hadrian came to Britain in the 2nd century and was responsible for the building of Hadrian's Wall.

Hafiz
From the Arabic, 'guardian'.

Haig
From the Anglo-Saxon, 'one who lives in an enclosure'. Best known for Field Marshal Lord Haig, the First World War general.

Hakim
From the Arabic, 'wise'.

Hakon
From the Old Norse, 'useful', it was the name of several Norwegian kings.
OTHER FORMS: Haakon, Hacon, Hak.

Hal
A short form of Henry.

Hale
From the Old English, 'healthy, whole'.
OTHER FORMS: Hal, Haley, Hally.

Hall
From the Old English, 'to cover', meaning a large, covered place.

Ham
From the Old English, 'home'. In the Bible Ham was one of the sons of Noah.

Hamilton
This name comes from a 13th-century English village and is the surname of a distinguished family who acquired the dukedome of Hamilton. In the US Alexander Hamilton was Treasury Secretary under George Washington.

Hamish

This is the anglicised form of Shamus, which is the Gaelic for James.

Hamlet

From the Old English, 'small village'. The indecisive hero of Shakespeare's play *Hamlet* is based on the Danish prince, Amleth.

Hamzah

Probably from the Arabic, 'lion', this was the name of the Prophet Muhhammad's uncle.
OTHER FORM: Hamza.

Hani

From the Arabic, 'joyful' or 'delighted'.

Hank

A short form of Henry.

Hannibal

The soldier from Carthage who crossed the Alps with his army and 37 elephants to fight the Romans.
OTHER FORMS: Annibal, Hanniball.

Hans

The German form of John.

Harald

The original form of Harold.

Harding

From the surname meaning 'hardy, strong'.

Hardy

From the Old French, 'brave, robust'.

Hari

From the Sanskrit, 'yellow-brown', is often applied to Vishnu or Krishna.

Harley

From the German, 'hemp field'. A favourite with bikers due to the Harley Davidson motorcycle.

Harold

From the Old German, 'army leader'. King Harold was killed by an arrow at the Battle of Hastings.
SHORT FORM: Harry.

Haroun

A variation of Aaron.

Harper

From the Old English, 'harp', a stringed musical instrument.

Harrison

From the surname meaning 'son of Harry'. Best known for the actor, Harrison Ford.

Harry

A short form of Harold and Henry.

Harte

From the Old English, 'mature male deer'.

OTHER FORMS: Hart, Hartman.

Hartley

From the Old English, 'deer meadow'.

Harun

A variation of Aaron and the name of a famous Arab caliph.

Harvey

From the French, 'battle-worthy'. The 6th-century St Harvey was a blind monk and wandering minstrel.

Hasan

From the Arabic, 'handsome' or 'good'. Al-Hasan was a grandson of the Prophet Muhammad.

OTHER FORMS: Hasin, Hussain, Hussein.

Hassan

A variation of Hasan.

Hastie

A short form of Hastings.

Hastings

From the Old Norse, 'house' or the Latin, 'spear'. The Battle of Hastings in 1066 was a victory for the Normans over the Anglo-Saxons.

SHORT FORMS: Hastie, Hasty.

Havelock

The Welsh form of Oliver.

Haven

From the Old English, 'harbour, refuge'.

Hayden

From the Old English, 'hay' and 'grassy dell'. It may also be in honour of the 18th-century composer Joseph Haydn.

OTHER FORMS: Haydn, Haydon.

Hector

From the Greek, 'hold fast', it was the name of the Trojan hero who was killed by Achilles.

OTHER FORMS: Ector, Ettore.

Hedley

From the Old English, 'heather' and 'meadow'.

Helmut

From the Old French, 'helmet' this name is mainly used in Germany.

Henri
French for Henry.

Henry
From the Old German, 'home ruler'. The name has been a favourite for English kings.
SHORT FORMS: Hal, Hank, Harry.

Hercule
The French form of Hercules. Best known through Agatha Christie's fictional detective Hercule Poirot.

Hercules
The mythical immensely strong son of Zeus, who performed 12 almost impossible tasks, 'The labours of Hercules', to gain immortality.

Herbert
From the Old German, 'bright army', it was the name of a saint who was Bishop of Cologne in the 11th century.
SHORT FORMS: Bert, Bertie, Herb, Herbie.

Herman
From the Old German, 'soldier'.
OTHER FORMS: Armand, Armin.

Hesketh
From the Old Norse, 'horse' and 'racecourse', this name came from various place names in northern England.

Hew
A variation of Hugh.

Hilaire
The French form of Hilary. Best known through the writer Hilaire Belloc.

Hilary
From the Latin, 'cheerful', this name is more usual for girls.
OTHER FORMS: Hilarius, Hillary.

Hildebrand
From the Old German, 'battle' and 'sword-blade'. St Hildebrand was another name for Pope Gregory VII.

Hiram
From the Hebrew, 'brother of the high one', it was the name of the King of Tyre in the Bible.

Holden
From the Old English, 'sheltered valley' or 'one who keeps watch'.
OTHER FORM: Holbrook.

Holt

From the Old English, 'wooded hill, copse'.

Homer

From the Greek, 'being led'. The Greek poet wrote the epics *The Iliad* and *The Odyssey*. A popular name in the US.

Horace

From the Roman family name Horatius, one of whom famously defended the bridge over the River Tiber.

Horatio

The first name of Lord Nelson, the British admiral, and of the fictional Hornblower in the novels by C.S. Forrester.

Howard

Possibly from the Scandinavian, 'high guardian'. It is the surname of a distinguished English family.
SHORT FORM: Howie.

Howell

Probably from the Welsh, 'eminent'.
OTHER FORMS: Howe, Hywel.

Howey

A variation of Howell.

Hubert

From the Old German, 'bright mind'. St Hubert is the patron saint of huntsmen.
SHORT FORM: Bert.

Hugh

From the Old German, 'heart' or 'soul', this name appears in the Domesday Book. St Hugh was the Abbot of Cluny monastery in France in the 11–12th centuries.
OTHER FORMS: Hew, Huey, Huw.

Hughie

A pet form of Hugh.

Hugo

The German form of Hugh.

Humbert

From the Old German, 'famous warrior'. The name of the narrator in Nabokov's novel *Lolita*.
OTHER FORMS: Hum, Humberto, Umberto.

Hunter

A surname now used as a first name.
SHORT FORM: Hunt.

Husayn

A variation of Hasan.

Hussain

A variation of Hasan.

OTHER FORM: Hussein.

Huw

A Welsh form of Hugh.

Huxley

From the Old English, 'field of ash trees'.

SHORT FORMS: Hux, Lee, Leigh.

Hyde

From the Old English, 'measure of land'. Hyde Park in London was one of King Henry VIII's deer parks before it was opened to the public.

Hywel

From the Welsh, 'eminent'.

OTHER FORMS: Hywell, Howell.

I ~ Girls

Ianthe
From the Greek, 'violet flower', this is a poetic name, which was used by Byron and Shelley.

Ida
From the Old German, 'hard work'. Gilbert and Sullivan used the name for the operetta *Princess Ida*, adapted from Tennyson's poem *The Princess*.
OTHER FORMS: Idena, Idina, Idony.

Idra
From the Aramaic, 'fig-tree' or 'flag'. The fig-tree was the symbol for a scholar for the Hebrews.

Ieasha
A variation of Aisha.
OTHER FORMS: Ieesha, Iesha

Ignatia
From the Latin, 'fiery', 'ardour', this is the female form of Ignatius.

Ilana
From the Hebrew, 'tree'.

Ilona
From the Hungarian, 'beautiful'. This is also a variation of Helen.

Imelda
From the Latin, 'wishful' this is the name of a little-known saint. It has a certain notoriety from the wife of the former President Marcos of the Philippines.

Imo
A short form of Imogen.

Imogen
From the Latin, 'likeness, imitation' this name appears in Shakespeare's *Cymbeline*.
SHORT FORMS: Immy, Imo.

Ina
This is an Irish version of Agnes, or a short form for names ending in 'ina' such as Georgina.
OTHER FORM: Ena.

India

The name of the sub-continent, which shows the interest there is in Indian culture. The granddaughter of the last Viceroy of India, Lord Mountbatten, was given the name.

SHORT FORM: Indy.

Indira

This Indian name is linked to the goddess Lakshmi, wife of Vishnu.

Inga

A variation of Inge and Ingrid.

Inge

From the Old Norse, 'meadow'. Ing was the god of fertility in Norse mythology.

OTHER FORMS: Ingaberg, Inger.

Ingrid

From the Old Norse, 'Inge's ride'. The god of fertility, Ing, rode a golden-bristled boar.

OTHER FORMS: Inga, Ingaborg, Ingrede.

Inés

The Spanish form of Agnes.

Inéz

A variation of Inés.

Iola

A variation of Iole.

Iolanthe

From the Greek, 'violet flower'. This is the name of a Gilbert and Sullivan operetta. The French form is Yolande.

Iole

From the Greek, 'dawn cloud'. The name of a Greek mythical princess with whom Hercules fell in love.

Iona

This is the name of a Scottish island used as a first name.

OTHER FORMS: Ione, Ionia.

Iphegenia

In Greek mythology she was the daughter of Agamemnon and was sacrificed to a goddess.

Irene

From the Greek, 'peace', she was the goddess of peace. The name can be pronounced with the emphasis on the first syllable or as three syllables.

OTHER FORMS: Eirene, Reenie.

Irina

The Russian form of Irene.

Iris

From the Greek, 'rainbow', the flower was named due to its bright colours. Iris was the messenger from the gods to mankind and used a rainbow as a bridge.

Irma

From the Old German, 'whole, entire'.
OTHER FORMS: Erma, Irmina, Irmintrude.

Isa

A short form of Isabel.

Isabel

Originally the Spanish form of Elizabeth and there are many variations of the name.
OTHER FORMS: Isa, Iseabel, Bella, Belle.

Isabella

The Latinate form of Isabel. It was the name of a queen of England, married to Edward II.

Isadora

From the Greek, 'gift of Isis'. Isis was the mythological Egyptian goddess of the moon and fertility. The name of Isadora Duncan, the dancer.
SHORT FORMS: Dora, Issy, Izzy.

Isbel

A variation of Isabel.

Iseabail

The Gaelic form of Isabel.

Iseult

A variation of Isolda.

Isha

A variation of Aisha.

Ishbel

A variation of Iseabail.

Isis

The Egyptian goddess of fertility.

Isleen

A variation of Aisling.

Isobel

A variation of Isabel.

Isola

From the Latin, 'isolated one'. This is the Italian word for an island.

Isolda

From the Welsh, 'fair one'. She was the beloved of Tristan in the medieval legend made famous by Wagner's opera.
OTHER FORMS: Iseult, Yseult, Ysolde.

Ita

Possibly from the Old Irish, 'thirst' or 'desire for truth'.

Iva

From the French, 'yew tree'.

Ivana

The female form of the Russian Ivan.

Iverna

This is the Latin name for Ireland.

Ivory

From the Welsh, 'highborn lady'.

Ivy

The name of the clinging plant and therefore signifying faithfulness.

I ~ Boys

Iain
The Scottish form of John.

Ian
A variation of Iain.

Ibrahim
The Arabic form of Abraham.

Idris
From the Welsh, 'ardent' and 'lord', this is a traditional Welsh name.

Idwal
From the Welsh, 'lord' and 'rampart'.

Iefan
A Welsh form of John.

Ieuan
The original Welsh form of John.

Ifan
A variation of Iefan.

Ifor
The Welsh form of Ivor.

Ignatius
From the Greek, 'fire'. The founder of the Jesuits, Inigo Lopez de Recalde, was known as St Ignatius of Loyala.
SHORT FORMS: Ignace, Ignaz, Inigo, Inigue.

Igor
The Scandinavian word for a hero.

Ike
A short form of Isaac. General Eisenhower the Second World War American hero was nicknamed Ike.

Illtyd
A Welsh name derived from 'land' and 'multitude' or 'ruler'.
OTHER FORM: Illtud.

Inderjit
From the Sanskrit, 'conqueror of the god Indra'.
OTHER FORM: Indrajeet.

Indra

Possibly connected with the Sanskrit 'raindrop' this is the name of the god of the sky and rain.

Inigo

A variation of Ignatius. Inigo Jones was a 16–17th century architect who introduced the Palladian style into Britain.

Ingmar

From the Norse, 'famous son'. Mainly used in Scandinavian countries.

Ingram

From the Old Norse, 'Ing's raven'. Ing was the god of peace and fertility.
OTHER FORMS: Ingo, Ingrim.

Innes

From the Gaelic, 'island'.
OTHER FORM: Innis.

Ior

The original version of Ifor and Ivor.

Ira

From the Hebrew, 'watcher'. A famous person who bore the name was the songwriter Ira Gershwin.

Irvin

An American variation of Irvine or Irving.

Irvine

From the Gaelic, 'handsome, fair'. Taken from the Scottish place name.

Irving

From the Scottish place name. Best known for the songwriter Irving Berlin.

Irwin

From the Old English, 'boar' and 'friend'. Mainly used in North America.

Isa

A short form of Isidor and Isaac.

Isaac

From the Hebrew, 'laughter', this biblical name was given to the son of Abraham and Sarah. It was the name of Sir Isaac Newton, the famous scientist.
OTHER FORMS: Izaak, Ike, Zak.

Isaiah

From the Hebrew, 'salvation of the Lord', it was the name of one of the major prophets.
OTHER FORMS: Is, Isaias, Issa.

Ishmael

From the Hebrew, 'God hears'. The name also means 'outcast' as he was thrown out of the house when his mother, Sarah, gave birth to Isaac.

Isidore

From the Greek, possibly 'gift of Isis'. The feminine form is Isidora.

SHORT FORMS: Isa, Izzy.

Ismael

The Arabic form of Ishmael. The Arabs can be known as Ismailites, descendants of Ismael.

Israel

From the Hebrew, probably 'may God prevail'. In the Bible the name was given to Jacob after he had wrestled with the angel and his descendants were named Israelites.

SHORT FORM: Izzy.

Ivan

The Russian form of John.

Ivar

From the Old Norse 'archer'.

Ivo

From the Old German, 'yew'. It was brought to Britain in the Norman Conquest; the French form is Yves.

Ivor

From the Welsh, 'lord'.

OTHER FORMS: Ifor, Iver.

Izaak

A variation of Isaac. Best known for Izaak Walton, the author of *The Compleat Angler*.

J ~ Girls

Jacaline
A variation of Jacqueline.

Jacinta
The Spanish equivalent of Hyacinth.

Jackalyn
A variation of Jacqueline.

Jackie
A short form of Jacqueline.
OTHER FORM: Jacky.

Jacoba
A female form of Jacob.

Jacobina
A diminutive of Jacoba.

Jacqueline
The French female form of Jacques, which is the equivalent of James or Jacob. Jacqueline Kennedy, the wife of the US President, made the name very popular in the 1960s.
SHORT FORMS: Jacki, Jackie, Jacqui.

Jacquelyn
A variation of Jacqueline.

Jacquetta
An Italian female form of Jacques.

Jade
The name for a gemstone of light green or blue. It became popular after the daughter of the rock star, Mick Jagger, was given the name.

Jaffa
From the Hebrew, 'beautiful', it is the name of a city in Israel. The oranges of the same name were originally grown near the city.
OTHER FORMS: Jafit, Yaffa, Yafit.

Jai
A variation of Jay.

Jaime
From the French, 'I love'.

Jaleesa

A newly formed name, probably made up of Jane and Lisa, it became popular through the TV programme *A Different World*.

Jalila

From the Arabic, 'glory' or 'greatness'.

Jalisa

A variation of Jaleesa.

Jamie

Although mainly a variation of James, this is used as a girl's name, particularly in the US.

Jamila

From the Arabic, 'lovely', this is a popular name in the Arab world. In France it can be found as Djamila.

Jan

A short form of Janet.

Jancis

Probably a combination of Jane and Frances. The TV wine commentator Jancis Robinson has made the name well known.

Jane

The female form of John, it probably derives from the French Jehane. The tragic Jane Seymour, third wife of Henry VIII, and the fictional Jane Eyre have been romantic bearers of the name. It is often coupled with another name as in Mary Jane or Sarah Jane.
OTHER FORMS: Janie, Jani, Jayne.

Janelle

A variation of Jane, which is more common in the US than in Europe.
OTHER FORM: Janella.

Janene

A variation of Janine.

Janet

First used in Scotland, this was derived from the French Jeanette, the femine of Jean.
OTHER FORMS: Jan, Janetta, Netta, Nettie.

Janette

A variation of Janet.

Janey

A variation of Jane.
OTHER FORM: Janie.

Janice

A variation of Jane.

Janine

Like Janet this was derived from the feminine of the French Jean.
OTHER FORM: Janina.

Janis

A variation of Janice.

Janna

An elaboration of Jan.

Japonica

Taken from the name of a red-flowered plant from Japan, which is part of the camellia family.

Jaqueline

A variation of Jacqueline.

Jaslyn

A blend of Jasmine and Lyn.

Jasmine

A sweet-smelling flower, which is used to make scent and to flavour tea.
OTHER FORMS: Jasmin, Yasmina, Yasmine.

Jawahir

From the Arabic, 'jewels'.

Jay

Probably a short form of any name beginning with J. It could also derive from the bird of the same name.
OTHER FORMS: Jai, Jaye.

Jayne

A variation of Jane.

Jazz

Usually a nickname for someone whose name begins with J. The word originated from the southern United States music scene.

Jean

This is the Scottish form of Jane, which derived from the French Jehane.
OTHER FORMS: Jenni, Jenny.

Jeana

A variation of Jean, mainly found in the US.

Jeanie

A pet form of Jean.
OTHER FORM: Jeannie.

Jeanette

A French version of Janet.

Jeanne

The French female form of John.

Jemima

From the Hebrew, 'dove', in the Bible this was the name of Job's eldest daughter. It was used by the Puritans in the 17th century.

SHORT FORMS: Jem, Jemma, Mima.

Jemma

A variation of Gemma, or a short form of Jemima.

Jenessa

A combination of Jennifer and Vanessa.

Jenna

A variation of Jenny.

Jenni

A variation of Jenny.

Jennifer

This is the Cornish form of Guenevere, from the Welsh, 'white ghost', the name of King Arthur's wife.

SHORT FORMS: Jen, Jenny.

Jenny

An old pet name for Jean, this is also a short form of Jennifer.

Jermaine

A variation of Germaine.

OTHER FORM: Jermain.

Jerry

A short form of Geraldine.

Jerusha

From the Hebrew, 'the perfect wife' this was a favourite with the Puritans.

Jess

A short form of Jessica.

Jessica

From the Hebrew, 'the rich one', this was the name given to Shylock's daughter by Shakespeare in *The Merchant of Venice*.

SHORT FORMS: Jess, Jessie, Jessye.

Jessie

From the Hebrew, 'riches'. A short form of Jessica and in Scotland it is a pet form of Janet or Jean.

Jessye

A short form of Jessica.

Jewel

Probably from the French, 'gemstone', this denotes someone who is very precious.

OTHER FORM: Jewell.

Jezebel

From the Hebrew, 'impure'. In the Bible this was the name of King Ahab's wife.

Jill

This is now often a name in its own right but is a short form of Jillian or Gillian.

Jillian

A variation of Gillian.
SHORT FORM: Jilly.

Jinny

A short form of Virginia.

Jo

A short form of Joanna and Josephine.

Joan

An old female form of John, this is a contraction of Johanna. Joan of Arc is a heroine of the French and was canonized in 1920.
OTHER FORMS: Joanie, Joni.

Joanna

Another female form of John, in the Bible it is the name of one of the followers of Jesus.
SHORT FORM: Jo.

Joanne

A development of the name Joanna it is sometimes spelt in two words, Jo Anne.
SHORT FORM: Jo.

Jocasta

The mother of Oedipus in the classical legend.

Jocelin

A variation of Jocelyn.

Jocelyn

There are several derivations for this name. One is the Latin, 'cheerful' or 'sportive', another is the Celtic name Josse, 'champion'.
OTHER FORM: Joscelin.

Jodie

Originally a short form of Judith, this is now used in its own right.
OTHER FORMS: Jodi, Jody.

Jodoc

The name of an early Breton saint.

Joe

A short form of Josephine.

Johanna

The Latin feminine form of Johannes, this came to England from France in the 12th century.

Joisse

A French form of Joyce.

Jolene
A modern combination name, which originated in the US.

Jolie
From the French, 'pretty one'.

Joni
A variation of Joanie.

Jonquil
A rare flower name, named after the type of narcissus.

Jordan
The name of a river in the Middle East, which means 'flowing down'. Christ was baptized in the river by John the Baptist and pilgrims used to bring back water from it to baptize their children.
OTHER FORMS: Jorden, Jordin, Jordyn.

Jorden
A variation of Jordan.

Jory
Short form of Marjorie.

Josceline
A variation of Jocelyn.

Josepha
A female form of Joseph.

Josephine
The French female form of Joseph. The name was made fashionable after the wife of the Emperor Napoleon.
OTHER FORMS: Fifi, Jo, Josie, Josephina.

Josette
A modern French form of Josephine.
OTHER FORM: Josetta.

Josie
Short form of Josephine.

Josse
An old form of Joyce.

Joy
From the French, 'joy'. The name was popular with the Puritans in the 17th century and now denotes the feelings of parents on seeing their new-born child.

Joyce
From the name of a 7th-century Breton saint, this was the name of some of William the Conqueror's followers. Nowadays it is rarely used as a man's name.
OTHER FORMS: Joy, Joycie.

Juanita
The Spanish form of Joan.
SHORT FORM: Nita.

Judi

A short form of Judith. Best known for the actress Judi Dench.

OTHER FORM: Judie.

Judith

From the Hebrew, 'a Jewess', this is the name of a book in the Apocrypha of the Bible. Judith saved the Israelites by cutting off the head of the enemy general, Holofernes.

SHORT FORMS: Judi, Judie, Judy.

Judy

A short form of Judith.

Julia

The female form of Julius, this was the name of several early saints. Giulia was its form when it first came to England from Italy.

Julian

The name was given to women as well as men until the Middle Ages. It is best known for the Blessed Julian of Norwich.

Juliana

The female form of Julian.

SHORT FORM: Julie.

Julie

The French form of Julia and the short form of Juliana.

Juliet

The short form of the Italian Giuletta, it probably became popular due to Shakespeare's *Romeo and Juliet*.

Juliette

The French form of Juliette.

June

From the name of the month.

Juniper

From the name of the plant, whose berries give flavour to gin and to many culinary dishes.

Juno

An Irish form of Una.

Justine

From the Latin, 'just', this is the female form of Justin and became popular due to Lawrence Durrell's novel of the same name.

OTHER FORM: Justina.

J ~ Boys

Jabez
From the Hebrew, 'sorrowful', this biblical name was popular with the 17th-century Puritans.

Jace
A short form of Jason.

Jack
Originally a pet name for John, this is now a name in its own right. It is also sometimes used as a pet name for James, perhaps influenced by the French Jacques.

Jackie
A pet form of Jack, but now more usually used for girls.

Jackson
Originally a surname this is more common in the US, in honour of President Andrew Jackson.

Jacob
From the Hebrew, 'follower' or 'supplanter'. In the Bible he was the father of 12 sons who gave their names to the 12 tribes of Israel and he had a famous dream where he saw a ladder with angels going up to heaven.
OTHER FORMS: Jacobus, Jake, Jock.

Jacques
The French form of Jack.

Jago
This is the Cornish form of James.

Jake
A name in its own right, but also a short form of Jacob.

Jalal
Arabic for 'glory' or 'greatness'.
OTHER FORM: Galal.

Jalil
Arabic for 'honoured' or 'revered'.
OTHER FORM: Galil.

Jaime

Spanish form of James.

James

From the Latin Iacomus, this was the name of two of Christ's Apostles. Many English and particularly, Scottish kings have borne the name. The Scottish form is Hamish and the Irish is Seamus.

SHORT FORMS: Jamie, Jim, Jimbo, Jimmy.

Jamie

The short form of James has become popular in its own right.

Jamal

From the Arabic, 'beautiful' this name is used by Black Muslims in the US.

OTHER FORM: Jamel.

Jaimal

A variation of Jamal.

Jamil

From the Arabic, 'handsome'.

Jan

A form of John used in such European countries as Holland and Poland, where it is pronounced 'Yan'.

Janus

From the Latin, 'passage, gateway'. The mythical Roman god of gateways who looked both ways, he gave his name to the month of January.

OTHER FORM: Januaris.

Japheth

From the Hebrew, 'beautiful'. In the Bible he was the youngest of Noah's three sons.

OTHER FORMS: Japhet, Yafet, Yaphet.

Jared

From the Hebrew, 'descent', according to the Bible he bore a son when he was well over 100 years old and lived on for a very long time.

OTHER FORMS: Jaron, Jarred, Jarrod.

Jarod

A variation of Jared.

Jaroslav

From the Czech, 'glory of spring', this is one of the most popular Czech names.

Jarrett

A variation of Garett.

Jarvis

A variation of Gervais.

Jason

The Greek form of Joshua. In Greek mythology he led the Argonauts to find the Golden Fleece. Best known for the Australian actor, Jason Donovan.
SHORT FORMS: Jace, Jay.

Jaspar

A variation of Jasper.

Jasper

This is a semi-precious stone of reddish brown quartz. Traditionally it is the name of one of the three kings who came to bring gifts to the infant Jesus.
OTHER FORMS: Caspar, Gaspar, Kaspar.

Jay

A pet form for names beginning with the letter J. It also comes from the noisy colourful bird.

Jed

A short form of Jedidiah, from the Hebrew, 'beloved of God'. This is more common in the US than in the UK.

Jedi

A variation of Jed.

Jeff

A short form of Jeffrey. Used as a first name mainly in the US.

Jefferson

From the surname of the third president of the US, Thomas Jefferson.

Jeffrey

A variation of Geoffrey.
Short form: Jeff.

Jem

A short form of Jeremy.

Jenkin

From the surname and a form of Jan, this is more usual in Wales.

Jeremiah

From the Hebrew, 'appointed by God', it was the name of the prophet who wrote the Book of Lamentations in the Bible.
OTHER FORMS: Hieronymous, Jeremias.

Jeremy

The Anglicized form of Jeremiah.
SHORT FORMS: Jem, Jerry, Jez.

Jermaine

A variation of Germaine, now quite common as a boy's name in the US.

Jerrell

A variation of Jeremy.
OTHER FORMS: Jerell.

Jerome

From the Hebrew, 'holy name'. The 4th-century St Jerome translated the Bible into Latin.

OTHER FORMS: Gerome, Geronimus, Gerry.

Jerry

A short form of Gerald, Gerard and Jeremy.

Jess

A variation of Jesse.

Jesse

From the Hebrew, 'gift', it was the name of King David's father in the Bible. Jesse James, the American outlaw and Jesse Jackson, the American politician are the best-known bearers of the name.

SHORT FORMS: Jake, Jess.

Jesus

From the Hebrew name Joshua, He was the Son of God in the Bible. It is popular in the Spanish-speaking world.

Jethro

From the Hebrew, 'excellence' or 'wealth', it is the name of the father-in-law of Moses. Recently it was the name of a character in the radio series *The Archers*.

SHORT FORMS: Jeth, Jett.

Jim

A short form of James.

Jimmy

A pet form of Jim.

Jo

A short form of Joseph.

Joachim

From the Hebrew, 'God will establish'. The alleged name of the father of the Virgin Mary, it is popular in continental Europe.

OTHER FORMS: Giachimo, Jochim, Joaquin.

Job

From the Hebrew, 'hated, oppressed'. A biblical character whose name is synonymous with patience.

OTHER FORMS: Jobey, Jobie.

Jocelyn

Originally a surname and used for boys, it is now more popular with girls.

SHORT FORM: Joss.

Jock

The Scottish version of Jack.

Jodi

A variation of Joe.

OTHER FORM: Jody.

Joe

A short form of Joseph.

Joel

From the Hebrew, 'Jehovah is God', it is the name of a minor prophet in the Bible. It is more common in the US.

Johan

From the Latin name Johannes.

John

From the Hebrew, 'God is gracious', it was the name of some of the most important men in the New Testament. The name of several saints, it has also been borne by 23 popes and is one of the most popular names in the world.
OTHER FORMS: Evan, Ian, Jack, Jon, Sean.

Johnnie

A diminutive of John.

Jolyon

A variation of Julian.

Jon

A short form of John and Jonathan.

Jonah

From the Hebrew, 'dove'. The story of Jonah and the whale in the Bible gave the name popularity in the Middle Ages.
Other forms: Jonas, Yona, Yonah.

Jonas

The Greek form of Jonah.

Jonathan

From the Hebrew, 'God's gift'. In the Bible David and Jonathan were devoted friends.
OTHER FORMS: Jon, Jonathon.

Jordan

From the River Jordan, whose name means 'flowing down'. Children baptized with water brought from the Holy Land were given the name.
OTHER FORMS: Jordain, Jordyn.

Jordon

A variation of Jordan.

Jorgen

Danish and German form of George.

Jos

A short form of Joseph or Josiah.

Joscelin
A variation of Jocelyn.

Joseph
From the Hebrew, 'God will add (another son)'. In the Bible he was the youngest son of Jacob and Rachel, who wore a coat of many colours. It is also the name of the husband of Mary, the mother of Jesus, and of Joseph of Arimathea, whose thorn staff grew into a tree at Glastonbury.
SHORT FORMS: Jo, Joe, Jos.

Joshua
From the Hebrew, 'the Lord saves'. In the Bible he succeeded Moses and led the Israelites into the Promised Land.
SHORT FORM: Josh.

Josiah
From the Hebrew, 'may the Lord heal'. The founder of the pottery firm, Josiah Wedgwood, made the name known.
SHORT FORMS: Josias, Jos.

Joss
A short form of Jocelyn.

Joubert
From the Old English, 'bright, shining'.
OTHER FORMS: Jovett.

Juan
The Spanish form of John.

Jubal
A biblical name, he was a descendant of Cain who invented the lyre and the harp.
SHORT FORM: Jube.

Jude
From the Hebrew name Yehudi, which means 'praise'. St Jude is the patron saint of lost causes.
OTHER FORMS: Jud, Judah, Judas, Judson.

Jule
A short form of Julius.

Jules
This is the French form of Julius and is common in France. It is also short for Julian.

Julian
From the Latin name Julianus, this probably comes from the Greek, 'soft-haired'. It was the name of numerous saints including St Julian the Hospitaller who helped poor travellers.
OTHER FORMS: Jolyon, Jules, Julyan.

Julius

Made famous by the conqueror of Britain and first Roman emperor, Julius Caesar.

SHORT FORM: Jule, Jules.

Julyan

A variation of Julian.

Jumbo

From the Swahili, 'elephant'. This started as a nickname.

Jun

From the Chinese, 'truth' and the Japanese, 'obedience'.

Junayd

From the Arabic, 'warrior'.

OTHER FORM: Junaid.

Junior

A name found in the US, meaning 'boy' or 'son'.

Junius

From the Latin, 'sacred to Juno'.

Jurgen

The German form of George.

Justin

From the Latin, 'just'. The 2nd-century Christian St Justin was martyred for refusing to sacrifice to the gods.

OTHER FORMS: Justinian, Justis, Jut.

Justino

A variation of Justin.

Justus

From the Latin, 'fair' or 'just'.

K ~ Girls

Kagami
From the Japanese, 'mirror', a reflection of the parents' love.

Kailey
A variation of Kayleigh.
OTHER FORM: Kaley

Kallie
A short form of Caroline.
OTHER FORM: Kally.

Kamala
From the Sanskrit, 'pale red', it is a name for the lotus flower. It is one of the Hindu goddess Lakshmi's names and is also a name for Shiva's wife.

Kamila
From the Arabic, 'complete' or 'perfect'.
OTHER FORM: Kamilah.

Kanisha
Fashionable amongst Afro-American parents, it is a modern version of Tanisha.
OTHER FORM: Quanisha.

Kanta
An Indian name meaning 'beautiful' and 'desired'.

Kara
The mythological Norse Valkyrie who took the form of a swan to follow her lover to war.
OTHER FORM: Cara.

Karena
A variation of Kara.

Karen
A Danish form of Katherine, which was introduced to America by Scandinavian settlers.
OTHER FORMS: Karan, Karin, Karyn.

Karenza
A variation of the Cornish Kerensa.

Karima
The female form of Karim.

Karin
A variation of Karen.

Karla
A female form of Karl or Carl.

Karma
From the Sanskrit, 'action' or 'effect'. In Hinduism this word signifies fate and destiny.

Karyn
A variation of Karen.
OTHER FORM: Karyna.

Kasia
A short form of Keziah and the Polish pet name for Katherine.

Kasimira
From a Slavonic word meaning 'commands peace', this is the female form of Kasimir.

Katharine
A variation of Katherine, this is the preferred spelling in the US and Germany.

Kate
A short form of Katherine. It was used by Shakespeare in *Taming of the Shrew* from which came the musical *Kiss me Kate*.
OTHER FORM: Cate, Katie, Katy.

Katelyn
An elaborate form of Kate.
OTHER FORM: Caitlin.

Katerina
The Russian form of Katherine.

Kath
A short form of Katherine.

Katha
A variation of Kathy.

Katherine
The name is associated with the Greek 'pure' and has been borne by many saints. There have also been at least three English queens with this name.
SHORT FORMS: Kate, Katie, Kay, Kitty.

Kathleen
The Irish form of Katherine.
OTHER FORMS: Cathleen, Caitlin.

Kathryn
A variation of Katherine.

Katrina
A variation of Catriona.

Katrine
A German form of Katherine.

Katy
A short form of Katherine.

Katya
The Russian pet form of Katerina.

Kay
A short form of Katharine, but also a name in its own right.
OTHER FORMS: Kai, Kaye.

Kayla
Probably a variation of Kayleigh.

Kayleigh
A modern invention, although it might have derived from the Irish surname.
OTHER FORMS: Kaylee, Kayley.

Keeley
From the Gaelic, 'beautiful girl', it is also a variation of Kayleigh or Kelly.
OTHER FORMS: Keelie, Keely.

Keighley
Another variation of Keeley.

Keisha
A popular name with Afro-American parents, it is possibly an adaptation of Aisha or Iesha.

Kelley
An Irish surname which means 'warlike', used for both sexes but usually for girls.
OTHER FORM: Kelly.

Kelsey
From the Old English, 'ship' and 'victory', this was originally a surname.

Kendall
Possibly from Kendal in Cumbria, this is taken from the surname.

Kendra
The female form of Kendrick.

Keren
From the Hebrew, 'horn of eye shadow' (the box containing kohl would have been made of horn), this is a short form of Kerenhappuch, the biblical daughter of Job.
OTHER FORMS: Keryn, Kerryn.

Kerena
A variation of Keren.

Kerensa
From the Cornish, 'affection, love'.
OTHER FORM: Kerenza.

Keri
A variation of Ceri

Kerry

From the Gaelic, 'dark one' this comes from the name of an Irish county. It seems to have originated in Australia.
OTHER FORM: Kerri.

Keshia

A variation of Kezia.

Kestrel

From the Old French, 'rattle', this is a bird's name occasionally used for girls.

Ketana

An Indian name for 'home'.

Kezia

A biblical name, it comes from the Hebrew for the spicey cassia tree.
SHORT FORMS: Kezzie, Kezzy, Kissie.

Keziah

A variation of Kezia.

Khadiya

From the Arabic, 'premature baby', this was the name of the first wife of the Prophet Muhammad.
OTHER FORMS: Khadeejah, Khadijah.

Kia

Possibly from the Maori greeting 'be well'.

Kiana

A modern invention found amongst Afro-Americans.

Kiara

This is a newly coined name which is popular with Afro-American parents.

Kiera

A female form of Kieran.
OTHER FORMS: Ciara, Ciera, Kiera.

Kim

Originally a short form of Kimberley this is now used in its own right.
OTHER FORM: Kym.

Kimberley

The name of a town in South Africa where there are diamond mines. It is more common in the US than in the UK.
OTHER FORMS: Kimberlee, Kimberlie, Kimberly.

Kimi

From the Japanese, 'sovereign', 'the best'.
OTHER FORMS: Kimie, Kimiko, Kimiyo.

Kirsten

Scandinavian form of Christine, popular in the English-speaking world.
OTHER FORM: Kiersten.

Kirsty
Scottish form of Christine or Kirstin.

Kismet
From the Arabic, 'destiny, fate'.

Kitty
A short form of Katherine.

Kizzie
A short form of Kezia.

Kodey
A variation of Codie.

Koko
From the Japanese, 'stork', a symbol of long life.

Koren
From the Greek, 'maiden'.
SHORT FORMS: Kora, Kori, Kory.

Korey
A variation of Corey.

Korrie
A variation of Corey.

Krista
A variation of Christa.

Kristeen
A variation of Christine.
OTHER FORMS: Kristene, Kristin, Kristine.

Kristie
A variation of Christie.

Kristina
The Swedish form of Christine.
OTHER FORMS: Krystyna.

Kryssa
A variation of Chrissa.

Kumari
From the Sanskrit, 'girl' or 'daughter'.

Kyle
From the Gaelic, 'narrow', this is a place name in Scotland.
OTHER FORM: Kyla.

Kylie
From an Aboriginal word meaning 'boomerang', popular due to the Australian actress Kylie Minogue.

Kym
A variation of Kim.

Kyrenia
From the Greek, 'lord'. Possibly from the name of the place in Turkish Cyprus.

K ~ Boys

Kahil
From the Arabic, 'friend, lover'.

Kaikane
From the Hawaiin, 'ocean'.
SHORT FORM: Kai.

Kalil
From the Greek, 'beautiful'.
OTHER FORMS: Kahlil, Kal, Kallie.

Kamal
From the Arabic, 'perfection'. In India it is a name for the lotus flower, from the Sanskrit, 'pale red'.

Kamil
From the Arabic, 'complete' or 'perfect'.

Kane
From the Gaelic, 'tribute', this is an Irish name.

Karel
A central European form of Carol, used for boys.

Karl
The German form for Charles.

Karim
From the Arabic, 'generous, noble'. One of the many names of God in the Koran.

Kashif
From the Arabic, 'discoverer'.

Kasimir
From the Slavonic, 'commands peace'.

Kaspar
A variation of Caspar and Jasper.

Kay
The name of one of the legendary Knights of the Round Table.
OTHER FORM: Kai.

Keane
From the Old English, 'wise, clever'.
OTHER FORMS: Kean, Keene, Kene, Kienan.

Keegan

This is an Anglicized form of a Gaelic surname.

Keir

A Scottish surname, it is best known for the first elected Labour MP, Keir Hardie.
OTHER FORM: Kerr.

Keiran

A variation of Kieran.

Keith

Probably from the Gaelic, 'wood', this was originally a Scottish surname.

Kelly

Originally an Irish name, possibly meaning 'strife', this is now more often a name given to girls.

Kelsey

From the Middle English, 'keel', this comes from a surname and is more common for girls.

Kelvin

The name of a Scottish river that runs through Glasgow, this is a transferred surname.

Kemp

From the Old English, 'warrior, champion', this is taken from the surname.

Ken

A short form of Kenneth.

Kendall

From the Old English, 'royal valley', this may come from Kendal in Cumbria.
Short forms: Kenn, Kennie, Kenny.

Kendrick

From the Old English, 'royal, ruler'. There are also Welsh and Scottish derivations.
OTHER FORM: Kenrick.

Kenelm

From the Old English, 'brave' and 'helmet'. A name known in England before the Norman Conquest.

Kennedy

From the Gaelic, 'royal and 'chief'. The name may be chosen because of the American President Kennedy, who was assassinated in 1963.
SHORT FORMS: Kenn, Kenny.

Kenneth

From the Gaelic, 'handsome'. Kenneth McAlpine was the first ruler of the Picts and the Scots in the 9th century.
SHORT FORMS: Ken, Kenny.

Kent

A surname, which comes from the English county and which probably derives from the Celtic, 'border'.

Kentigern

From the Gaelic, 'chief lord'. An early Scottish saint of the name was nicknamed Mungo. He is the patron saint of Glasgow.

Kenton

Taken from various place names in the UK, this is also a surname.

Kenward

From the Old English, 'brave' and 'guard'.

Kermit

From the Dutch, 'church'. The name is best known for the cartoon character Kermit the frog in a television programme.

Kerr

A transferred surname from the north of England.

Kerry

From the Irish county of the same name. A popular name, which originated in Australia.
OTHER FORMS: Kerri, Kerrie.

Kester

A Scottish form of Christopher.

Ketan

An Indian name meaning 'home'.

Kevin

From an old Irish name meaning 'handsome birth'. The 6th-century St Kevin is one of the patron saints of Dublin.
OTHER FORMS: Kev, Kevan, Keven.

Kieran

A variation of the Irish name Ciaran, 'dark-haired'. This name has been borne by many saints and is very popular.
OTHER FORMS: Cieran, Kieron, Kyran.

Killian

The name of various early Irish saints, it is the Anglicized form of the Gaelic Cillian.
OTHER FORM: Kilian.

Kim

A short form of Kimberley, it is often used in its own right. It was used by Rudyard Kipling for the hero of his novel *Kim*, set in India.

Kimball

Possibly from Cymbeline, the 1st-century English chieftain.
SHORT FORMS: Kim, Kimmie, Kimmy.

Kimberley

The name of a town in South Africa, this was briefly popular for boys as a commemoration of the Boer War.
SHORT FORMS: Kim, Kimbo.

King

More usual in the US, from the word for a monarch. The civil rights leader Martin Luther King made it popular with Afro-Americans.

Kingsley

From the Old English, 'king's meadow', it has become known through the novelist Kingsley Amis.
OTHER FORMS: Kingsleigh, Kinsey.

Kip

A short form of Kipling, but also used independently.
OTHER FORM: Kippy.

Kipling

Possibly from the Old English, 'smoked herring', this was the surname of the novelist Rudyard Kipling who wrote the *Jungle Books*.
Short forms: Kip, Kippy.

Kiran

From the Sanskrit, 'ray of light, sunbeam'.

Kirk

From the Norse, 'church', particularly used in Scotland. The name became popular due to the filmstar Kirk Douglas.
OTHER FORMS: Kirkland, Kirtland, Kirtly.

Kile

A variation of Kyle.

Kishen

A variation of Krishna.

Kistna

A variation of Krishna.

Kit

A short form of Christopher.

Klaus

A Germanic short form of Nicholas.

Knute

The Danish King Knute ruled England in the 10th century and the legend was that he could control the waves.

OTHER FORMS: Canute, Knud, Knut.

Krishna

From the Sanskrit, 'black', this is the name of a Hindu god.

OTHER FORMS: Kishan, Kistna, Krishan.

Kumar

From the Sanskrit, 'boy', this is more generally thought to mean 'prince'.

Kurt

A short form of Conrad or Konrad.

Kushal

An Indian name, which means 'clever'.

Kyle

From the Gaelic, 'narrow strait'.

OTHER FORMS: Kile, Ky.

L ~ Girls

Lacey
Originally taken from the surname, the first name now has associations with 'lace'. It is particularly popular in the US.

Lachina
A female form of Lachlan.

Laeta
A form of Letitia.

Laetitia
A variation of Letitia.

Laila
From the Persian, 'night' or 'dark-haired'.
OTHER FORMS: Laili, Laleh, Layla.

Lakeisha
A name used by Afro-American parents, as a variation of Keisha.

Lakshmi
From the Sanskrit for 'mark' (birthmark), this is the name of the goddess of good fortune.

Lalage
From the Greek, 'to chatter', this is pronounced 'lal-a-dgee' or 'lal-a-ghee'. The name of a character in John Fowles' *The French Lieutenant's Woman*.
SHORT FORMS: Lal, Lallie, Lally.

Lalita
An Indian form of endearment from the Sanskrit, 'charming'.

Lally
A short form of Lalage.

Lana
A short form of Alana.

Laquisha
A variation of Lakeisha.

Laraine
Possibly from the French, 'the queen'. A variation of Lorraine.

Lara
The Russian short form of Larissa.

Larch

From the name of the tree.

Lark

From the tiny bird which has a sweet song. One of several birds' name which became current in the 20th century.

Lashay

A variation of Lakeisha.

Lashonda

A variation of Lakeisha.

Latasha

A recently invented name in the US, especially amongst Afro-American parents.
OTHER FORM: Latisha.

Latrice

A variation of the boy's name Patrice, mainly found in the southern US.

Latoya

A name invented by the mother of the singer LaToya Jackson.
OTHER FORMS: Latonya, LaToy, Toyah.

Laura

From the Latin, 'bay tree, laurel'. The name of a martyred 9th-century saint.
OTHER FORMS: Lolly, Lora, Lori.

Laurain

A variation of Lorraine.

Laureen

A variation of Lauren.

Laurel

From the name of the tree, probably influenced by Laura.
OTHER FORM: Lorel.

Lauren

A variation of Laura.
OTHER FORMS: Laurene, Loren.

Laurencia

The female form of Laurence.

Lauretta

A diminutive of Laura.

Laurissa

A variation of Laura.

Lavender

From the sweet-smelling flower which is used to make scent.

Laverne

From the French, 'spring-like'.

Lavinia

The mythological wife of Aeneas, her name came to mean 'woman of Rome'.
SHORT FORMS: Vin, Vina, Vinnie, Vinny.

Lavina

A variation of Lavinia.

Layla

From the Persian, 'night'.

Lea

From the Old English, 'meadow' it is also short for Leah.

Leah

From the Hebrew, 'languid'. In the Bible she was married to Jacob although he wanted to marry her sister Rachel.
OTHER FORMS: Lea, Lia.

Leanne

A variation of Lianne.

Leanora

A variation of Leonora, it is also spelt Leonore.

Leda

A mythical queen of Sparta who was seduced by Zeus in the form of a swan.
OTHER FORMS: Lida, Lidia.

Lee

Taken from the surname meaning 'meadow'. Now widely popular with both sexes.

Leena

An Indian name meaning 'devoted'.
Other form: Lina.

Leigh Ann

A variation of Lianne.

Leila

From the Persian, 'night'. A variation of Laila, it was used in a romantic poem by Lord Byron.
OTHER FORMS: Leilah, Lila.

Lena

A diminutive of such names as Caroline, Eleanor and Helena. The name of the singer Lena Horne.
OTHER FORMS: Leena, Lenette, Lina.

Lenore

A variation of Leonora.

Leola

A female version of Leo.

Leona

A female version of Leo.

Leonie

A female version of Leon, derived from the French, 'lion'.
OTHER FORMS: Leola, Leontine.

Leonora

A variation of Eleanor, this is the name given by the composer Beethoven to one of his overtures.
OTHER FORM: Leonore.

Lesley

From the Scottish surname, the name of a Scottish noble family.
OTHER FORMS: Les, Lesly.

Leslie

A variation of Lesley. Best known for the French actress Leslie Caron.
OTHER FORMS: Les, Lesli.

Letitia

From the Latin, 'joyfulness', this is a more modern spelling of Laeticia.
OTHER FORMS: Leticia, Lettice, Letty, Tiesha.

Lettice

The Anglicized form of Laeticia, this name was popular with the Victorians.
SHORT FORMS: Lettie, Letty.

Leverne

A variation of Laverne.

Lia

The Italian form of Leah.

Lianne

Probably from the French Eliane, this can also be spelt Leanne.
OTHER FORMS: Lee Ann, Leigh Ann.

Libby

A short form of Elizabeth, supposed to be a pet name for Queen Elizabeth II.

Liberty

From the Latin, 'freedom'.

Liese

A German diminutive of Elizabeth.

Liesel

A European diminutive of Elizabeth.

Lilac

From the Persian, 'indigo, blue' this is the name of a shrub with delicately scented blooms.

Lilian

A variation of Lillian.

Lillian

From the Latin, 'lily', the name may originally have been a diminutive of Elizabeth.

OTHER FORMS: Lila, Lillah, Lilla.

Lily

The name of the flower, whose trumpet-shaped blossoms are a symbol of purity.

SHORT FORM: Lil.

Lilith

From the Hebrew, 'belonging to the night'. Lilith was the mythical evil wife of Adam before Eve.

OTHER FORMS: Lilis, Lilita, Lillith.

Lillias

A variation of Lillian.

Lin

A short form of Linda.

Lina

A diminutive of names ending in '-lina', it is also from the Arabic, 'tender'.

Linda

Possibly from the Spanish, 'pretty', but also as a diminutive of such names as Belinda or Rosalinda.

SHORT FORMS: Lin, Lindy.

Linden

The name of the lime or linden tree.

Lindsey

An old Scottish family name, borne by the Earls of Crawford.

OTHER FORMS: Linsay, Linsey, Linzi.

Lindy

A short form of Linda.

Linet

A variation of Lynette.

OTHER FORM: Linette.

Linnet

From the name of the small songbird, and also a variation of Lynette.

Lisa

A short form of Elizabeth.

Lisette

French form of Elizabeth.

Liz

A short form of Elizabeth.

Liza

A short form of Elizabeth.

Lizzy

A diminutive of Liz.

Lo
A short form of Dolores or Lois.

Lois
From the Greek, 'good, desirable' this is a biblical name. Pronounced 'lo-is' or in the French way 'loy'.
SHORT FORM: Lo.

Lola
A short form of Dolores, which is used in Spanish-speaking countries.

Lolita
A diminutive of Lola, this is best known through Vladimir Nabokov's novel which was also made into a film.

Lolly
A short form of Laura.

Lora
From the Latin, 'thin wine made from grapeskins'. Also a short form of Laura.

Loreen
A variation of Lora.
OTHER FORM: Lorene.

Lorel
A variation of Laurel.

Lorelei
From the German, 'song'. The cliff from which a mythical siren sang to lure sailors onto the rocks.
OTHER FORMS: Lurleen, Lurlene.

Loren
A variation of Lauren.

Loretta
A diminutive of Laura.

Lorinda
A variation of Lora.

Lorna
An invention for the heroine of R.D. Blackmore's novel *Lorna Doone*, probably taken from Lorne, in Scotland.
OTHER FORM: Lorne.

Lorraine
The name of the district in France, this is a transferred surname.
OTHER FORMS: Laraine, Lauraine, Loraine, Lori.

Lottie
A diminutive of Charlotte.
OTHER FORM: Lotty.

Lotus

The name of a plant, the fruit of which in Homer's *Odyssey* made whoever ate it drowsy and indolent.

Louie

A short form of Louise or Louisa.

Louella

A modern name derived from Louise. It is associated with the American gossip columnist Louella Parsons.

SHORT FORM: Lou.

Louisa

The Latin female form of Louis.

SHORT FORM: Lulu.

Louise

The French female form of Louis. The 17th-century saint helped to found the charity, St Vincent de Paul, which helps the ailing poor.

SHORT FORMS: Lou, Louie.

Lourdes

Taken from the major pilgrim site in France, where the sick go in hopes of a miraculous cure.

Love

From the Old English, 'tender affection'.

Loveday

A name originally given to babies born on the day set aside to settle quarrels, now mainly used in Cornwall.

OTHER FORM: Lowdy.

Lowena

From the old Cornish name 'joy'.

OTHER FORMS: Lowenek, Lowenna.

Luba

From the Russian, 'love'.

Lucasta

A variation of Lucia.

Lucetta

An Italian variation of Lucia.

Lucette

A French form of Lucy.

Lucia

From the Latin, 'light', the name is current in Italy.

Lucilla

The diminutive form of Lucia, the name was borne by several early saints.

Lucille

The French form of Lucilla, used also mainly in the US.

Lucina

From the Latin, 'light'. The goddess was the patron of childbirth, symbolically bringing babies into the light.

Lucinda

Another derivative of Lucy, this is the name of the heroine in Peter Carey's Australian novel *Oscar and Lucinda*.

Lucretia

A female form of the Roman family name. Best known because of the alleged poisoner Lucretia Borgia.

Lucy

From the Latin, 'light'. The martyrd St Lucy is the patron saint of people with diseases of the eye.
OTHER FORMS: Luce, Lulu.

Ludmilla

From the Slavonic name meaning 'people' and 'grace'. A Bohemian saint of the name was the grandmother of St Wenceslas.
OTHER FORMS: Milla, Millie.

Luella

A variation of Louella, particularly popular in the southern US.

Luned

A short form of Eluned.

Lydia

From the Greek, meaning 'lady from Lydia', a kingdom in Asia Minor. The Bible tells of St Paul's stay in the widow Lydia's house when he converted her to Christianity.
OTHER FORM: Lyddie.

Lyn

A short form of Carolyn and Lynette.
Other forms: Lin, Linn, Linne.

Lynda

A variation of Linda.

Lynette

A variation of Luned.

Lynn

A variation of Lyn.
OTHER FORMS: Lynne.

Lyris

From the Greek, 'lyre', which is a musical instrument like a harp.

Lysandra

The female form of Lysander.
SHORT FORMS: Sandra, Sandie.

L ~ Boys

Lacey
The name of a powerful Irish family in the Middle Ages, which originally came from a French place name.
OTHER FORM: Lacy.

Lachlan
A Scottish name possibly meaning 'warlike'. It was brought over by the Vikings.
SHORT FORMS: Lachie, Lochie.

Laertes
The Greek mythological father of Odysseus. Known in the UK from Shakespeare's play *Hamlet*, where it is the name of Ophelia's brother.

Lal
From the Sanskrit, 'caress', in Hindi it means 'beloved'.

Lambert
From the Old German, 'bright, shining', it is the name of a 7th-century saint from Holland.
SHORT FORMS: Bert, Bertie, Lammie.

Lamont
From the Norse, 'law man'. An Irish and Scottish surname this is used as a first name mainly in the US.

Lance
A short form of Lancelot.

Lancelot
From the Latin, 'lance'. Sir Lancelot was a Knight of the Round Table at the legendary court of King Arthur and fell in love with Queen Guinevere.
OTHER FORM: Launcelot.

Landan
From the Old English, 'long hill'.

Landon
A variation of Landan.

Lane
From the Old English for a narrow pathway between banks or hedges.
OTHER FORMS: Lanie, Leney.

Lang
From the Old English, 'long', 'tall'.

Langdon
From the Old English, 'long town'.

Langford
From the Old English, 'wide river crossing'.

Langley
From the Old English, 'long pasture'.

Larrie
A short form of Laurence or Lawrence.

Larry
A short form of Laurence or Lawrence.

Lars
A Scandinavian form of Laurence.

Latham
From the Old English, 'land that is owned'.
SHORT FORMS: Lathe, Lay.

Latimer
From the Old English, 'land by the sea'.
SHORT FORMS: Lattie, Latty.

Launcelot
A variation of Lancelot.

Laurence
A name associated with the laurel plant, a symbol of victory. There were several saints who bore the name, including St Laurence O'Toole, a 12th-century Irish Archbishop of Dublin.
SHORT FORMS: Larrie, Larry, Laurie.

Laurie
A short form of Laurence.

Lawrence
A variation of Laurence made famous by the writer D.H. Lawrence and the romantic 'Lawrence of Arabia'.
SHORT FORMS: Larry, Lawrie, Loren.

Lawrie
A short form of Lawrence.
OTHER FORM: Lowrie.

Lawson
A transference of the surname, regularly used in Australia.

Lawton
From the Old English, 'hill town'.

Laz
A pet form of Larry.

Leal
From the Anglo-Saxon, 'loyal' or 'faithful'.

Leander

From the Greek, 'lion' and 'man'. The mythological Greek hero who fell in love with Hero; when he was drowned she threw herself into the sea to be with him.
SHORT FORMS: Lea, Lee, Leo.

Leary

The Anglicized form of the Gaelic for 'calf herd', the name was borne by several early Irish saints and kings.

Lee

From the Old English, 'meadow', this name is popular in the US, possibly in honour of General Robert E. Lee.

Leeland

From the Old English, 'sheltered land'.
OTHER FORMS: Leighland, Leland.

Lee Roy

A variation of Leroy, popular with Afro-Americans.

Leigh

A variation of Lee.

Leighton

A place name in England, from the Old English, 'settlement'.

Lem

A short form of Lemuel.

Lemuel

From the Hebrew, 'devoted to God'. It was the name of Jonathan Swift's hero in *Gulliver's Travels*.
SHORT FORMS: Lem, Lemmy.

Len

A short form of Leonard.

Lennan

From the Gaelic, 'darling, sweetheart'.

Lenny

A short form of Leonard.
OTHER FORM: Lennie.

Lennard

A variation of Leonard.

Lennon

Used as a first name in honour of John Lennon, the Beatles singer.

Lennox

From the Scottish surname, also the name of an earldom and the first name of the British composer Sir Lennox Berkeley.

Leo
From the Latin, 'lion'. Many saints, emperors and popes bore the name.

Leolin
A variation of Llewelyn.
OTHER FORM: Leoline.

Leon
The French form of Leo.

Leonard
From the Old German, 'strong as a lion', it was the name of a 5th-century saint who was patron of prisoners.
SHORT FORMS: Len, Lenny

Leonardo
The Italian form of Leonard. Best known for Leonardo da Vinci, who painted the Mona Lisa.

Leopold
From the Old German, 'people' and 'bold'. It has been the name of several Belgian kings.

Leroy
From the French, 'the king'. This is popular amongst Afro-Americans.
OTHER FORMS: Elroy, Lee, Lee Roy, Roy.

Les
A short form of Leslie.

Leslie
Possibly from the Gaelic, 'garden of hollies', this is taken from the surname of the Scottish clan who were earls of Rothe.
SHORT FORM: Les.

Lester
A contraction of Leicester, the name of the city, it is transferred from the surname. Known through Lester Piggott, the jockey.
SHORT FORM: Les.

Levi
From the Hebrew, 'associated'. A biblical name of the Apostle Matthew, the name is mainly Jewish.

Lewie
A variation of Louis or a pet form of Lewis.

Lewis
From the Old German, 'famous warrior'
SHORT FORMS: Lew, Lewie.

Lex
A short form of Alexander.

Liam

A short form of William, it has been popular due to a pop star and a footballer of the same name.

Lindsay

From the place name of Lindsey in Lincolnshire, meaning 'the wetland'. Also used for girls, when it is more commonly spelt Lindsey.

Linford

From the Old English, 'flax' or 'lime tree' and 'ford' (river crossing). Best known for the athlete Linford Christie.

Linton

From the Old English, 'flax' or 'lime tree' and 'enclosure'.

Linus

A Latin form of the Greek name, it was the name of the second pope. In modern times it is associated with the character in the cartoon *Peanuts*.

Lionel

From the French, 'young lion'. The name of one of the legendary Knights of the Round Table.

Livingstone

From the Old English, 'from Lief's town'. A surname used as a first name in the US.

Llew

From the Welsh, 'lion'.

Llewellyn

From the original Welsh name Llywelyn, derived from the Welsh, 'lion'. The name was borne by two great Welsh princes. Other forms: Fluellen, Leoline, Llywelyn.

Lloyd

From the Welsh, 'grey', the name is a transferred surname.
OTHER FORMS: Floyd, Loy.

Llywelyn

A variation of Llewellyn.

Logan

A Scottish place name, also used as a surname. James H. Logan crossed a blackberry with a raspberry to create a loganberry.

Lon

A short form of Lonnie.

Lonnie

Possibly an Anglicized version of the Spanish Alonso, it is associated with Lonnie Donegan, the singer.

SHORT FORM: Lon.

Lorcan

An Anglicized form of a Gaelic name, which was borne by an Irish saint, the 12th-century Archbishop of Dublin.

Loredo

From the Italian town Loreto, where the Virgin Mary's house was supposedly moved in the 13th century.

Lorimer

From the Latin, 'harness-maker'.

SHORT FORM: Lori.

Lorne

Mainly found in the US, this name may come from the Scottish district.

Lou

A short form of Lewis and Louis.

Louis

The Old French Clovis, the name of the first French king, became transmuted to Louis, which was the name of many of the later French monarchs.

SHORT FORMS: Lou, Louie.

Lowell

From the Old English, 'love, praise'.

OTHER FORMS: Loyal, Loyte.

Lovell

From the Old French, 'wolf-cub'.

Loyal

From the Latin, 'faithful', mainly used in the US.

SHORT FORM: Loy.

Lucas

The Latin form of Luke meaning a man from Lucanius, a town in Italy.

Lucian

The Anglicized form of Lucius.

Lucien

The French form of Lucian.

Lucius

From the Latin, 'light'.

Ludo

A short form of Ludovic.

Ludolf

From the Old German, 'famous wolf'.

Ludovic

From the Latin form of Louis, Ludovicus.

SHORT FORM: Ludo.

Luke

The Anglicized form of Lucas. The Gospel writer, St Luke, is the patron saint of doctors and painters.

Lute

A short form of Luther.

Luther

From the Old German, 'people' and 'army'. The name is best known for Martin Luther who started the Reformation and founded the Lutheran church, and for the civil rights leader Martin Luther King.

Lyall

A transferred surname, possibly meaning 'from the island'.

Lyn

A short form of Llewellyn or a male form of Lynne.

OTHER FORM: Lynn.

Lyndon

From the Old English, 'lime tree' and 'hill'. Associated in the US with President Lyndon Baines Johnson.

Lysander

From the Greek, 'the liberator'.

SHORT FORM: Sandy.

M ~ Girls

Mab
A short form of Mabel. Queen Mab is the name of the fairy who brings dreams to the sleeper.

Mabel
From the Latin, 'worthy of love', this was originally Amabel. A popular name with the Victorians, it has since gone out of fashion.
SHORT FORM: May.

Maybelle
With Maybelline, a variation of Mabel.

Mackenzie
From the Scottish surname, this is more usual in the US when used as a girl's name.
OTHER FORMS: Makensie, Makenzie.

Maddy
Short form of Madeleine or Madison.

Madeleine
The French form of Magdalene, which was taken from St Mary Magdalene.
OTHER FORMS: Madelaine, Madelin(e), Madge.

Madelon
A variation of Madeleine.

Madge
A pet name for Margaret.

Madhur
The Hindi for 'sweet'.

Madison
From the surname, this is used for both sexes in the US.
SHORT FORMS: Maddie, Maddy.

Madonna
From the Italian name for the Virgin Mary, it is particularly popular due to the filmstar of the same name.

Mae
A variation of May.

Maegan

A variation of Megan, the Welsh form of Margaret.

Maeve

The Anglicized form of the legendary Irish Meadhbh, Queen of Connacht.
OTHER FORMS: Mave, Meave, Meaveen.

Magdalene

The name of Mary Magdalene (the woman from Magdala) the biblical sinner who bathed Christ's feet and was forgiven her sins.
OTHER FORMS: Mag, Magdalen.

Magda

A short form of Magdalene, more common in continental Europe.

Maggie

A short form of Margaret, also spelt Maggy.

Magnolia

A flower name taken from the creamy pink blossom of the magnolia tree.

Mahalia

From the Hebrew, 'tenderness', this is best known through the singer Mahalia Jackson.

Mahina

From the Hawaiian, 'moon'.

Mahira

From the Hebrew, 'speed, energy'.

Maia

The name of the Roman goddess who was the mother of Jupiter and Mercury.
OTHER FORM: Maya.

Maida

From the Old English, 'maiden', a young unmarried girl.
OTHER FORMS: Maidie, Maidey.

Maidie

An affectionate nickname for a young girl, which is used in its own right.

Mair(e)

The Welsh form of Mary.

Mairi

The Gaelic form of Mary.

Mairin

A variation of Maureen.

Maisie

A particularly Scottish pet form of Margaret.

Mallory

From the French, 'unfortunate', this is a transferred surname more used in the US.
SHORT FORMS: Mallie, Mally.

Malvina

Based on the Gaelic, 'smooth brow', this comes from an 18th-century fictional name. Las Malvinas, the Spanish name for the Falkland islands comes from the port of St Malo in Brittany.

Mamie

From the French, 'my sweetheart', this is also a pet form of Margaret.

Manda

A short form of Amanda.

Mandy

A pet form of Amanda.

Manisha

An Indian name for someone who is intelligent.

Manju

From the Sanskrit, 'beautiful'.
OTHER FORMS: Manjuba, Manjulika

Manon

A French variation of Mary, known through Massenet's opera *Manon*.

Mara

From the Hebrew, 'bitter', this is a biblical name.

Marcella

A female form of Marcel, this was the name of a 4th-century Roman saint.
OTHER FORMS: Marcelle, Marcelline.

Marcia

A female form of the Latin Marcius. St Marcia was rather an obscure early martyr.
OTHER FORMS: Marcie, Marcine, Marcy, Marsha.

Marcy

A short form of Marcia.

Margaret

From the Latin, derived from the Greek, 'pearl'. A lovely early belief was that oysters looked at the moon by night and caught a drop of dew in their shells which was transformed into a pearl by the moonbeams. The name of several saints, especially the daughter of Edmund Ironside of England who was the wife of King Malcolm of Scotland.
SHORT FORMS: Daisy, Maggie, Meg, Peg(gy).

Margaretta

A variation of Margarita.

Margarita

A Spanish form of Margaret.

Margery

Originally a pet form of the French name Marguerite.

SHORT FORMS: Marge, Margie.

Marghanita

A variation of Margarita.

Margot

A French short form of Margaret.

Margoletta

A variation of Margaret.

Marguerite

The French form of Margaret and the name of the flower, the ox-eye daisy.

Mari

The Welsh form of Mary.

Maria

The Latin form of Mary, originally a variation of Miriam.

Mariamne

Thought to be closer to the original form of the name of the Virgin Mary.

OTHER FORMS: Mariam.

Marian

A short form of Marie or a combination of Mary and Ann.

OTHER FORM: Marion.

Marianne

A French variation of Marian, this is the name given to the French Republic.

Marianna

The Spanish form of Marianne.

Marie

The French form of Maria, this is pronounced with the stress on the last syllable.

Mariella

An Italian diminutive of Maria.

SHORT FORM: Mariel.

Marietta

An Italian diminutive of Maria.

SHORT FORM: Mariette.

Marigold

The name of the yellow and orange flower, named for its gold colour.

Marilene

A variation of Marilyn.

Marilyn

A combination of Mary and Lyn. Well known for the luscious filmstar Marilyn Monroe.

OTHER FORMS: Marilynn, Marylin.

Marina

From the Latin, 'of the sea', it was the name of an early saint. A Greek princess of the name married the Duke of Kent in the 1930s.

Marisa

A modern variation of Mary.

OTHER FORMS: Marie, Marissa.

Marjorie

An alternative spelling of Margery, and associated with the herb marjoram.

SHORT FORMS: Marje, Marjie.

Marlene

A contracted form of Mary Magdalene. Best known for the German actress Marlene Dietrich and for the song *Lili Marlene* which was popular during the Second World War.

OTHER FORMS: Marlee, Marlena.

Marsha

A variation of Marcia.

Martha

From the Aramaic , 'lady'. In the Bible she is the sister of Mary, who sat and listened to Christ's stories while Martha did all the chores and complained about it.

SHORT FORMS: Marta, Marthe, Mattie.

Martina

The female form of Martin. Best known for the tennis player Martina Navratilova.

Martine

The French form of Martina.

Marty

A short form of Martina and Martine.

OTHER FORM: Marti.

Marvel

From the Latin, 'full of wonder'.

Mary

A biblical name, meaning 'dew of the sea'. The name of the mother of Jesus. A recent trend is the linking of Mary with another name, such as Mary-Rose or Mary-Grace.

Mat(h)ilda

From the Old German, 'mighty in battle'. It was the name of the wife of William the Conqueror.
SHORT FORMS: Matty, Tilly.

Matty

A short form of Matilda.

Maud

An old French or German form of Matilda, this was the name of the daughter of King Henry I of England. Popular in the 19th century after Tennyson's poem of the same name.
OTHER FORMS: Maude, Maudie.

Maura

A variation of Maire, the Irish form of Mary.

Maureen

An Anglicized version of Mairin, 'little Mary'.
SHORT FORM: Mo.

Mauve

From the French, 'lilac-coloured'.

Mave

A variation of Maeve.

Mavis

From the Old French, 'song thrush'.

Maxime

A French female form of Max.

Maxine

A female form of Max, which is short for Maximilian.
SHORT FORMS: Maxie, Maxy.

May

From the name of the month and of the hedgerow shrub, it is also a short form of Margaret and Mary.
OTHER FORMS: Mae, Mai.

Maya

The Indian name comes from the Sanskrit, 'illusion'. The European form is a variation of Maia.

Maybelle

A variation of Mabel.
OTHER FORM: Maybelline.

Meadhbh

From the Gaelic, 'she who makes drunk'.
OTHER FORM: Maeve.

Meave

A variation of Maeve.
OTHER FORM: Meaveen.

Meera

An Indian name meaning 'saintly woman'.

Meg

A short form of Margaret, mainly Scottish.

Megan

The Welsh form of Meg, it is widely used beyond Wales.
OTHER FORMS: Maegan, Maygen, Meghan.

Mehetabel

From the Hebrew, 'God makes happy', it is a biblical name. Made known through the cat of the name in the poems *Archy and Mehitable*.
OTHER FORM: Mehitabel.

Mehul

An Indian name referring to 'rain clouds'.

Meirion

A Welsh form of Maria.

Melanie

From the Greek, 'black' or 'dark', it was the name of two 5th-century saints.
SHORT FORMS: Mel, Melly.

Melantha

From the Greek, 'dark flower'.

Melicent

A variation of Millicent.
OTHER FORM: Melisent.

Melinda

From the Greek, 'bee' or 'honey'.
SHORT FORM: Mindy.

Melisande

The French form of Millicent.
OTHER FORMS: Melisenda.

Melissa

From the Greek, 'bee', it was the name of a mythical nymph.
OTHER FORM: Melit(t)a.

Melloney

Variations of Melanie.
OTHER FORMS: Meloney, Mellonny.

Melody

From the Greek, 'song', this is a modern coinage.

Melvina

A variation of Malvina.

Mercedes

From the Spanish, 'Our Lady of the Mercies'.
SHORT FORM: Mercy.

Mercia

An old form of Mercy, from the old Anglo-Saxon kingdom of the same name.

Mercy

From the Latin, 'reward', this is one of the virtues, another name for Charity.
SHORT FORM: Merry.

Meredith

From the Welsh surname meaning 'lord', this is now a first name for girls as well as boys.
SHORT FORM: Merry.

Meriel

A variation of Muriel.

Merle

From the French, 'blackbird', this was the name of an American filmstar, Merle Oberon.

Merrill

A variation of Muriel.

Merry

A short form of Mercy and Meredith.

Meryl

A variation of Muriel, best known for the actress Meryl Streep.

Meta

A pet form of Margarita.

Mha(i)ri

The Gaelic form of Mary.

Mia

The Scandinavian short form of Mary, well known for the actress Mia Farrow.

Michaela

French female form of Michael.

Michelle

The female form of the French Michel.

Mignonette

From the French, 'little darling', it is also the name of a sweet-smelling flower.
SHORT FORM: Mignon.

Mildred

From the Old English, 'gentle strength', this was the name of a 7th-century saint.
SHORT FORMS: Millie, Milly.

Milla

A short form of Camilla.

Millicent

From the Old German, 'strength' and 'work'. The French version was Melisande or Melusine.
SHORT FORMS: Millie, Milly.

Millie, Milly

Short forms of Mildred, Camilla and Millicent.

Mima

A short form of Jemima.

Mimi

A pet form of Maria, mainly used in French-speaking countries.

Mimosa

From the Latin, 'imitative', this is the name of the feathery yellow blossomed shrub.

Mindy

A short form of Melinda.

Minna

A short form of Wilhemina.
OTHER FORM: Minnie.

Minta

A short form of Araminta.
OTHER FORM: Minty.

Mira

A variation of Myra.

Mirabelle

From the Latin, 'wonderful'. This is also taken from the sweet plum-like fruit.
OTHER FORMS: Mirabel, Mirabella.

Miranda

From the Latin, 'admirable', it was used by Shakespeare for the heroine in *The Tempest*.
SHORT FORMS: Mirrie, Mirry.

Mireille

A French name probably derived from the Provencal 'to admire'.

Miriam

A biblical name derived from the Hebrew name Maryam. It was the name of a sister of Moses.
SHORT FORMS: Mirrie, Mitzi.

Mitzi

A short form of Miriam.

Missy

A pet form of Miss, and more common in the southern US.

Mo

A short form of Maureen or Morwenna.

Mohana
From the Sanskrit, 'attractive', a female form of one of the names of Krishna.

Moira
An Anglicized form of the Gaelic Maire (Mary).
OTHER FORM: Moyra.

Moirin
A variation of Maureen.

Molly
A short form of Mary.

Mona
The Anglicized form of the Gaelic for 'noble', possibly connected to the Greek, 'single'.

Monica
Possibly derived from the Latin, 'to advise'. St Monica was the mother of St Augustine and a model mother.
Short forms: Mona, Monna.

Mor
From the Gaelic, 'great' or 'large', this was a very common name in medieval Ireland.

Morag
A pet form of Mor, this is now popular in its own right.

Moreen
A variation of Maureen.

Morgan
From the Welsh male name. The best known female of the name was the legendary Morgan le Fay, the wicked stepsister of King Arthur.

Morna
A variation of Myrna, this is mainly Irish or Scottish.

Morven
From the district on the west coast of Scotland, it means 'high peak' in Gaelic.

Morwenna
A Cornish and Welsh name which probably means 'maiden'. There are churches in Cornwall dedicated to the 5th-century saint of the same name.
SHORT FORMS: Mo, Morwen.

Moyra
A variation of Moira.

Muadhnait
From the Gaelic, 'noble' or 'good', this is Anglicized to Mona.

Muirne
From the Gaelic, 'beloved'.

Munira
From the Arabic, 'brilliant', the female form of Munir.

Murali
From the Sanskrit, 'flute'.

Muriel
An old Celtic name, which means bright sea. It was brought to England during the Norman Conquest.
OTHER FORMS: Meriel, Murial.

Myfanwy
From the Welsh, 'my fine one'.
SHORT FORMS: Fanny, Myfi.

Myra
A name invented in the 17th century and used mainly in poetic works.
OTHER FORM: Mira.

Myriam
A variation of Miriam, more common in France.

Myrna
From the Arabic, 'myrrh', the name of a strongly scented substance.

Myrtle
A Greek name from the flowering shrub, which was a symbol of love in the 19th century.

M ~ Boys

Mac
From the Gaelic, 'son'.
OTHER FORM: Mack.

Macbeth
From the name of the Scottish king made famous by Shakespeare's play.

Mackenzie
From the Scottish surname, meaning 'son of Coinneach'.

Macsen
A variation of of Maximilian.

Madoc
From the Welsh, 'fortunate'.
OTHER FORM: Madog.

Magnus
From the Latin, 'great', this was the name of seven Norwegian kings and some early saints.
OTHER FORM: Manus.

Malcolm
From the Gaelic name meaning 'servant of St Columb'. It was the name of four Scottish kings.
SHORT FORMS: Mal, Colm, Colum.

Malik
From the Arabic, 'master'.

Malory
From the surname and also the French, 'wild duck'.

Manfred
From the Old German, 'peace'.
Other forms: Manifred, Mannie, Manny.

Manish
An Indian name meaning someone who is intelligent.

Manley
From the surname, meaning 'guardian of the fields'.

Manny
A short form of Emanuel.

Mansur
From the Arabic, 'helped by God'.

Manuel
Spanish form of Emanuel.

Manus
A variation of Magnus

Maol Mhuire
From the Irish, 'devotee of Mary'. The English variation is Miles.
OTHER FORM: Mael Moire.

Marc
French form of Marcus.

Marcel
French form of the Latin Marcellus.

Marcus
From the name of the Roman god of war, Mars, who also gives his name to the month of March.

Maredudd
Old Welsh form of Meredith.

Mario
Italian form of Marius.

Marius
Possibly from the Roman god, Mars.

Mark
From the Latin, Marcus, this is the name of the writer of one of the four New Testament gospels. It is also the name of several other early saints.
OTHER FORMS: Marco, Marcos, Marcus.

Marlin
From the Old English, 'sea'.
OTHER FORMS: Marle, Marlo.

Marlon
Possibly derived from the French Marc, with 'lon' added, it first appeared as the name of the actor Marlon Brando.
OTHER FORMS: Marlin, Marlo.

Marlow
A variation of Marlin and a transferred surname.
OTHER FORM: Marlowe.

Marmaduke
From the Irish name, 'servant of Madoc'.
SHORT FORM: Duke.

Marquis
From the French, 'ruler of the marches' (frontier districts). The English Marquess is an aristocratic rank.

Marshall

From the Old French, 'groom', it later became the name of an official of the royal household who was responsible for state occasions.

SHORT FORM: Marsh.

Martin

From the Latin name Martinus, derived from the war god Mars. St Martin of Tours was a 4th-century saint.

OTHER FORMS: Martyn, Marti.

Marty

A short form of Martin, also used as an independent name.

Marvin

A variation of Mervin.

Marx

A German form of Mark.

Mason

From the surname given to a worker in stone. Especially used in the US.

Masud

From the Arabic, 'lucky'.

Mathew

A variation of Matthew.

Matthew

From the Hebrew, 'gift of God'. It is the name of one of the writers of the four gospels in the New Testament.

SHORT FORM: Matt.

Matthias

The Greek form of Matthew, it was the name of the disciple in the Bible who was chosen to take the place of Judas Iscariot.

OTHER FORMS: Mathias, Matt.

Maurice

From the Latin implying someone dark or swarthy. The name of a 3rd-century saint who was martyred in Switzerland, this French spelling of the name is now used widely outside France.

SHORT FORM: Maurie.

Max

A short form of Maximilian or Maxwell.

Maximilian

From the Latin, 'greatest', it was the name of two early saints. Maximilian I was Emperor of the Holy Roman Empire in the 15th century.

OTHER FORMS: Max, Maxie, Maxy.

Maxwell

From the Scottish surname meaning 'Mac's well', it is more common in Canada.

SHORT FORMS: Mac, Max.

Maynard

From the Old German, 'strong' and 'powerful'.

Other forms: May, Mayne, Menard.

Mel

A short form of Melville and Melvin.

Melchior

From the Hebrew, 'king'. He was one of the three kings who brought gifts to the infant Jesus.

Melville

From the Scottish surname, this is used particularly in the US.

Short form: Mel.

Mercer

From the surname meaning a trader. The name of an 18th-century US general.

Meredith

From the old Welsh, 'great chief'.

SHORT FORM: Merry.

Meredydd

Old Welsh form of Meredith.

Merlin

From the Welsh name Myrddin, 'sea fort'. The name of the legendary King Arthur's wizard.

OTHER FORMS: Marlin, Merle, Merlene, Merlyn.

Merrick

From the Old English, 'ruler of the sea'.

Mervyn

From the Welsh, 'sea fort'.

OTHER FORMS: Marvin, Mervin.

Meurig

Welsh form of Maurice.

Michael

From the Hebrew, 'who can be like God?' He was one of the Archangels and the patron saint of battles.

SHORT FORMS: Mike, Mick, Micky.

Micah

The name of a 17th-century biblical prophet.

SHORT FORM: Mica.

Michel

French form of Michael.

Miguel
Spanish form of Michael.

Milan
From the Czech, 'grace', best known for the novelist Milan Kundera. The Indian name comes from a word meaning 'union'.

Miles
Possibly from the Old German, 'gentle', brought to England by the Normans.
OTHER FORMS: Milo, Myles.

Milo
Latinate form of Miles.

Milton
From the Old English, 'village mill'. Also the name of the 17th-century poet John Milton who wrote *Paradise Lost*.

Mischa
Russian form of Michael.
OTHER FORM: Misha.

Mitchell
From the surname, an Anglicized form of Michel.
SHORT FORM: Mitch.

Mohammad
A variation of of Mohammed and Muhammad.

Mohan
From the Sanskrit, 'attractive'. An early name of Krishna.

Monroe
From the Scottish and French, 'wheel turner', this is a transferred surname.

Montague
From the aristocratic surname deriving from the French, 'pointed hill'.
OTHER FORMS: Montagu, Monte, Monty.

Monty
A short form of Montague.

Moray
A variation of Murray.

Morcant
From the Welsh, 'brilliant', the early form of Morgan.

Mordecai
From the name of the god Marduk who was the Babylonian god of life and fortune.
SHORT FORMS: Mord, Mort, Morty.

Morgan

From the traditional Welsh name Morcant.

Morien

From the Welsh, 'sea-born', another early form of Morgan.

Morrie

A short form of Morris.

Morris

From the Latin, 'a Moor', meaning dark-skinned. This is the English form of Maurice.

SHORT FORM: Morrie.

Mortimer

From the aristocratic surname, which derives from the French, 'dead sea'.

SHORT FORMS: Mort, Morty.

Moses

A biblical name given to the prophet who led the Israelites to the promised land and received the Ten Commandments from God.

OTHER FORMS: Moyse, Moss.

Mostyn

From the Welsh place name.

Muhammad

From the Arabic, 'praise'. The name of the Prophet of Islam, it is very popular and is spelt in several ways.

OTHER FORMS: Moha(m)med, Moha(m)mad.

Muhsin

From the Arabic, 'benevolent' or 'charitable'.

Muir

From the Scottish surname connected to the word 'moor'.

Muneer

A variation of Munir.

Mungo

From the Gaelic, 'beloved'. St Kentigern, who was bishop of Glasgow, was known as St Mungo. Mungo Park explored the River Niger in the 18th century.

Munir

From the Arabic for 'illuminating'.

OTHER FORM: Muneer.

Munroe

A variation of Monroe.

OTHER FORM: Munro.

Murdoch

From the Gaelic, 'sailor'.

SHORT FORM: Murdo.

Murray

From the Scottish surname, derived from the district of Moray.

OTHER FORMS: Murrie, Murry.

Murtaugh

From the Irish, 'skilled sailor'.

SHORT FORM: Murty.

Mustafa

From the Arabic, 'chosen'. One of the names for the Prophet Muhammad.

Myles

A variation of Miles.

Myrddin

Welsh form of Merlin and Mervyn.

Myron

From the Greek, 'fragrant', it was the name of several early saints.

Short forms: My, Ron, Ronny.

N ~ Girls

Nadia
From the Russian, 'hope'.
OTHER FORMS: Nada, Nadie, Nadiya.

Nadine
A French form of Nadia.
OTHER FORMS: Nada, Na(d)dy.

Nafisa
From the Arabic, 'precious' or 'delicate'.
OTHER FORMS: Nafeesa, Nafisah.

Naima
From the Arabic, 'comfortable, tranquil'.
OTHER FORM: Naeema.

Nan
A short form of Ann or Nancy.

Nancy
Originally a pet form of Ann, but long used in its own right.
OTHER FORMS: Nan, Nance, Nanci(e).

Nana
A French form of Nancy.

Nanette
The diminutive of the French form of Nancy.

Nanny
A pet form of Anne or Nancy.

Naomi
From the Hebrew, 'delightful, pleasant'. In the Bible Naomi was the loving mother-in-law of Ruth.
SHORT FORMS: Nae, Naome, Nomi.

Narelle
From an aboriginal word or name, this is mainly found in Australia.

Nastasia
A short form of Anastasia.

Natalie
From the Latin, 'birthday', especially the day of Christ's birth.
OTHER FORMS: Nattie, Nathalie, Tally.

Natalya

The Russian form of Natalie, also from the Latin, 'birthday'. St Natalya gave help to Christian martyrs in the 4th century.
SHORT FORMS: Talia, Talya.

Natasha

The Russian pet form of Natalya.
OTHER FORMS: Natacha, Natasja, Tasha.

Nayana

From the Sanskrit, 'eye', given to girls with beautiful eyes.

Neha

An Indian name meaning 'rain'.

Nell

A short form of Eleanor, Ellen or Helen. Well known because of King Charles II of England's mistress Eleanor (Nell) Gwyn.
OTHER FORMS: Nellie, Nelly.

Nerissa

Possibly from the Greek, 'sea-sprite', this name became known because of Portia's maid in Shakespeare's *The Merchant of Venice*.

Nerine

From the Nereids, who were sea nymphs who attended the sea god Neptune.

Nerys

A Welsh name, perhaps meaning 'lordly'.
OTHER FORMS: Nerida, Nerissa.

Nessa

A traditional Gaelic name and also a variation of Agnes and a short form of Vanessa.
OTHER FORMS: Nesha, Nessie.

Nesta

Welsh form of Agnes.
OTHER FORM: Nest.

Netta

A Latin version of Nettie.

Nettie

A pet form of Annette, Janet and Jeannette.

Neva

From the Spanish, 'snow', 'white'.

Niamh

Pronounced 'nee-av' or 'neev', this is from an Irish word meaning 'brightness'. In the legend she was a goddess who fell in love with the son of Finn MacCool and took him to the land of perpetual youth.

Nicci

A short form of Nicole or Nichola.

Nichola

The female form of Nicholas.
SHORT FORMS: Nickie, Nikki.

Nickie

A short form of Nichola.

Nicola

An Italian form of Nicholas, taken in the English-speaking world as the female form.

Nicole

The French female form of Nicholas.
SHORT FORMS: Nic, Niccie.

Nicoletta

The Italian diminutive of Nicola.

Nicolette

The French diminutive of Nicola.

Nigella

A female form of Nigel.
OTHER FORM: Nigelia.

Nikita

Originally a Russian boy's name, from the Greek, 'unconquered'. Also an Indian name derived from, 'the earth'.

Nikki

A short form of Nicola, used as a name in its own right.

Nile

From the River Nile in Egypt, this is more popular with Afro-Americans.
OTHER FORM: Niles.

Niloufer

An Indian name meaning 'celestial one'.
OTHER FORM: Neelofar.

Nina

Originally a Russian short form of names ending in 'nina', but now a popular name in its own right.

Nisha

An Indian name derived from the word 'night'.

Nishant

An Indian name meaning 'the end of the night'.

Nita

A short form of Anita or Juanita.

Noelle

The female form of Noel, it is a name often given to children born at Christmas time.

Nola

The female form of Nolan.
OTHER FORMS: Noleen, Nolene.

Nona

From the Latin, 'ninth', in Victorian times it was given to the ninth child, if a daughter. Also a short form of Anona, the Welsh form of Anne.

Nora

A mainly Irish name, the short form of names such as Honoria and Leonora.
OTHER FORMS: Nonie, Nore.

Norah

A variation of Nora.

Noreen

An Anglicized form of the Irish Noirin, a diminutive of Nora.

Norma

Possibly from the Latin, 'standard, rule' and a female form of Norman. The name became popular due to Bellini's opera *Norma*.

Nova

From the Latin, 'new'. It is the name of a star that becomes very bright for a time.

Nuala

A short form of the Irish Fionnuala, meaning 'white-shouldered'.

Nureen

From the Arabic, 'light'. The wife of the mighty Moghul Emperor, Shah Jehan was called Nur.

Nyree

The Anglicized form of a Maori name, known through a New Zealand filmstar, Nyree Dawn Porter.
OTHER FORM: Ngaire.

N ~ Boys

Nadim
From the Arabic, 'friend'.
OTHER FORM: Nadeem.

Naeem
A variation of Naim.

Nafis
From the Arabic, 'precious'.

Nahum
From the Hebrew, 'consoling', it was the name of a biblical prophet.
SHORT FORM: Nemo.

Naim
From the Arabic, 'comfortable' or 'contented'.
OTHER FORM: Naeem.

Nairn
From the Celtic, 'one who lives by the alder tree'.

Namir
From the Arabic, 'leopard'.

Nandy
A short form of Ferdinand.

Napoleon
From the Greek, 'new town'. Napoleon Bonaparte, the French emperor, was the most famous bearer of the name.
SHORT FORMS: Leon, Nap.

Nat
A short form of Nathan or Nathaniel.

Nathan
From the Hebrew, 'gift'. The name of a prophet in the Bible who carried God's reproaches to King David, who had married Bathsheba after having her husband killed.
SHORT FORM: Nat.

Nathaniel
From the Hebrew, 'God's gift '. The name of one of the 12 Apostles in the Bible, also known as Bartholomew.
SHORT FORMS: Nat, Nate.

Nayan
From the Sanskrit, 'eye'.

Neal
A variation of Neil.

Ned
A short form of Edward.
OTHER FORM: Neddy.

Neil
From the Gaelic, 'champion' or 'cloud'. Its early use was mainly in Ireland and Scotland, but is now used more widely.

Neirin
A short form of Aneurin.

Nelson
This means 'Neil's son'. Used as a first name in honour of Horatio Nelson, the English admiral who destroyed the French fleet at the Battle of Trafalgar.

Nemo
From the Greek, 'from the glen'. Also a short form of Nahum.

Nestor
The mythical king who was at the siege of Troy. The name is associated with wisdom and long life.

Neville
From the French, 'new town', this comes from the surname of the powerful Neville family.
OTHER FORM: Nevile.

Newell
From the Latin, 'new, young'.
OTHER FORM: Nowell.

Newton
From the Old English, 'new settlement', this is a transferred surname. Best known for the English scientist, Sir Isaac Newton.
SHORT FORM: Newt.

Niall
The Irish form of Neil.

Nicholas
From the Greek, 'people's victory'. St Nicholas is the patron saint of children and sailors and gave his name to Santa Claus, the bringer of Christmas presents.
SHORT FORMS: Nick, Nicko, Nicky.

Nick
A short form of Nicholas.
OTHER FORM: Nicky.

Nico
A short form of Nicholas.

Nicol

A variation of Nicholas in the Middle Ages, now being revived.
OTHER FORMS: Nicoll, Nichol(l).

Nigel

From the Old Latin name Nigellus, 'dark, night'.
SHORT FORMS: Nige, Nye.

Nikhil

From the Sanskrit, 'complete, entire'.

Ninian

Mainly Scottish, this was the name of a 5th-century saint who converted the Picts to Christianity.
OTHER FORMS: Nennian, Ninidh.

Noah

From the Hebrew, 'rest', the biblical name of the man who filled his Ark with pairs of animals to survive the Flood.
SHORT FORM: Noe.

Noble

From the Latin, 'renowned, famous'.

Noel

From the French, 'Christmas', this name is often given to children born on Christmas Day.
OTHER FORM: Nowell.

Nolan

From the Irish surname, or a form of Northland, meaning 'from the north'.
OTHER FORM: Noland.

Noll

A pet form of Oliver.

Norbert

From the Old French, 'north' and 'bright'. St Norbert founded an order of monks in France in the 12th century.
SHORT FORMS: Bert, Bertie, Norb, Norby.

Norman

From the Old English, 'man from the north'. The Normans from northern France invaded England in the 11th century.
SHORT FORMS: Norm, Normie, Norrie.

Norton

From the surname meaning 'north settlement' in Old English.

Nowell

A variation of Noel.

Nye

A short form of Aneurin, it became well known due to the Labour politician 'Nye' Bevan.

O ~ Girls

Obelia

From the Greek, 'pointer, needle', this derives from the tall stone pillars first used in Egypt.

SHORT FORMS: Belle, Belia.

Octavia

The female form of the Roman family name Octavius, meaning 'eighth'.

OTHER FORMS: Octavie, Ottavia, Tavie.

Odelia

From the Greek, 'song'. Odes were originally long poems which were sung at festivals.

OTHER FORMS: Odelie, Odilla.

Odessa

The female form of Odysseus.

Odette

The female form of the German Odo, meaning 'prosperous', it was the name of a famous Second World War resistance heroine.

OTHER FORMS: Detta, Odetta.

Odile

From the feminine of the German, 'wealthy', this is a French name. The 8th-century saint founded a convent in Alsace.

OTHER FORMS: Odilia, Odilon.

Ofra

From the Old English, 'present, gift'.

Ola

From the Norse, 'descendant', meaning the daughter of a chieftain.

Oleander

A flower name from the evergreen shrub, which has pink, white or red blossoms.

Olga

From the Norse, 'holy', this was the name of a Russian saint in the 10th century who helped to spread Christianity.

OTHER FORMS: Helga, Olia, Ollie, Olva.

Olia

A variation of Olga, mainly used by people of Russian descent.

Oliva

The name of the patron saint of olive crops.

Olive

From the Mediterranean tree whose fruit is pressed to make olive oil. The branches are symbols of peace.
OTHER FORMS: Ol, Ollie.

Olivia

The female form of Oliver, associated with the olive tree. The name was used by Shakespeare for the heroine in his play *Twelfth Night*.
SHORT FORMS: Livia, Liv(v)y, Oliva.

Olwen

From the Welsh, 'fair footprint'. She was a legendary character whose footsteps were covered in white clover.

Olwyn

A variation of Olwen.

Olympia

This name comes from Mount Olympus in Greece, which was the legendary home of the gods.
OTHER FORMS: Olimpe, Olimpia, Olympias.

Oona

An Anglicized form of the Gaelic name Una.
OTHER FORMS: Oonagh.

Opal

From the Sanskrit, 'precious stone'. The name of a pale gemstone containing fiery streaks, believed by some to be very lucky and by others to be the opposite.
OTHER FORMS: Opalina, Opaline.

Ophelia

From the Greek, 'help'. Best known for the poor mad girl in Shakespeare's play *Hamlet*.
OTHER FORMS: Ofelia, Ofilia, Ophelie.

Ophrah

From the Hebrew, 'fawn', in the Bible it is a man's name. The American chat show hostess has made the variation Oprah well known.
OTHER FORMS: Ofra, Ophra, Oprah.

Orchid

A flower name from the exotic, rare species found in grassland or in trees in tropical countries. The name signifies luxury.

Oriel

From the Latin, 'gold', it is also the name of an Oxford college.

Oriole

From the Latin, 'golden bird'. The golden oriole is a bird which has bright yellow plumage.

Orla

From the Irish, 'golden princess'.
OTHER FORMS: Orlagh, Orlaith.

Orpah

The name of Ruth's sister-in-law in the Bible. Probably derived from the Hebrew, 'female deer'.

Osyth

A 7th-century saint and queen of the East Saxons who founded a nunnery in Essex.

Ottilie

From the Old German, 'wealth'. The saint of the same name is the patron saint of Alsace.
OTHER FORM: Ottilia.

Ottoline

A diminutive of Ottilie, this was the name of a literary hostess in the early 20th century, Lady Ottoline Morell.

O ~ Boys

Obadiah
From the Hebrew, 'servant'. The name of a prophet in the Bible.
OTHER FORMS: Obediah, Obe, Obie.

Oberon
The king of the fairies in Shakespeare's *A Midsummer Night's Dream*.
OTHER FORMS: Auberon.

Octavius
From the Latin, 'eighth', this was a Roman family name. It is traditionally given to the eighth child in a family.
OTHER FORMS: Octave, Octavio, Otavio.

Odell
From the Old German, 'prosperity'.
SHORT FORMS: Dell, Ode, Odie.

Odilo
A French saint who was Abbot of Cluny in the 11th century.

Odin
The mythical Norse god of creation, wisdom and art.

Odo
From the Old German, 'wealthy'. St Odo was the second Abbot of Cluny in France and the name was brought to Britain by the Normans.
OTHER FORMS: Oddo, Otho, Otto.

Odysseus
The name of the hero in Homer's epic poem the *Odyssey*.

Oengus
An old Irish form of Angus.

Offa
The King of Mercia who ruled most of England south of the Humber and was responsible for building Offa's Dyke.

Ogden
From the Old English, 'oak' and 'valley'. Best known for the poet Ogden Nash who wrote humerous verse.
OTHER FORM: Ogdan.

Oisin
The Irish form of Ossian.

Ollie

A short form of Oliver.
OTHER FORM: Ol, Olly.

Olaf

From the Norse name meaning 'ancestor, remains'. King Olaf I of Norway was a saint and there have been several other kings of the name in Norway.
OTHER FORMS: Olav, Olif.

Oleg

A Russian male form of Olga.

Oliver

From the same source as Olaf, although it could also be derived from the olive tree, the sign of peace. Two famous bearers of the name were Oliver Cromwell and the hero of Dickens' novel *Oliver Twist*.
SHORT FORMS: Ol, Ollie, Olly.

Omar

From the Arabic, 'long life', it is the name of the 11th-century Persian poet Omar Khayyam and of the filmstar and bridge player Omar Sharif.

Orde

From the Latin, 'regular, ordered'.
OTHER FORM: Ordell.

Oran

From the Gaelic, 'pale-skinned', this was the name of a 6th-century Irish saint.

Oren

From the Hebrew, 'tree' this name is mainly found in the US.
OTHER FORMS: Orin, Orren, Orrin.

Orestes

From the Greek, 'mountain'. He was the son of Agamemnon in Greek mythology.
OTHER FORMS: Orest, Oreste.

Orlando

The Italian form of Roland. A character in Shakespeare's *As You Like It*.
SHORT FORMS: Lanny, Orlan, Orley.

Ormond

From the Norse, 'serpent' or the Old French, 'elm tree'.
OTHER FORMS: Orman, Ormand.

Orson

From a French diminutive of the Latin, 'bear'. Best known through the actor Orson Welles.

Orville

A name made up by the novelist Fanny Burney. The first name of one of the Wright brothers, pioneers of flying.

Osbert

From the Old English, 'bright' and 'god', it was more used at the beginning of the 20th century.
SHORT FORMS: Oz, Ozzie.

Oscar

From the Old English, 'god' and 'spear'. A name given to Ossian's son in the Fenian sagas. It is known through the poet and playwright Oscar Wilde and as the name of the trophy awarded by the American Academy of Motion Pictures.
OTHER FORMS: Ossie, Ossy, Ozzie, Ozzy.

Oskar

Scandinavian version of Oscar.

Osman

The western form for the Turkish name Usman.

Osmund

From the Old English, 'protected by God'. The Norman St Osmund was involved in the Domesday Book and the building of Salisbury Cathedral.
OTHER FORMS: Osmand, Osmond.

Ossian

From the Irish name Oisin, 'little deer'. The legendary son of Finn MacCool.
OTHER FORM: Osheen.

Oswald

From the Old English, 'god of the wood'. The name of two English saints, one of whom was the Bishop of Worcester and Archbishop of York in the 10th century.
SHORT FORMS: Oz, Ozzie, Ozzy.

Otis

From the Greek, 'ear', this is a transferred surname, found mainly in the US.
OTHER FORM: Otes.

Otto

A short form of the German meaning 'wealth', 'prosperity'. There was a 12th-century saint of the name. King Otto the Great was Emperor of the Holy Roman Empire and it is a name used by several other royal Germanic families.

Owen

A very popular Welsh name, which may be the Welsh form of Eugene. Owen Glendower, who fought to make Wales independent from the English, was one of the most famous name bearers.
OTHER FORMS: Ewan, Ewen, Owain, Owayne.

Oz

From the Hebrew, 'strength'. Also a short form of Osbert and Oswald.
OTHER FORMS: Ozzie, Ozzy.

P ~ Girls

Padma

From the Sanskrit, 'lotus', this name is associated with the goddess Lakshmi.
OTHER FORMS: Padmal, Padmavati, Padmini.

Page

A variation of Paige.

Paige

From the surname, meaning a young attendant. It gained popularity in the US due to its use for television characters and is now gaining ground in the UK.

Pallas

From the Greek, 'knowledge' it was the name for the goddess of wisdom, Pallas Athene.

Palma

From the Latin, 'palm tree'. The palm branch was a symbol of victory.
OTHER FORMS: Palmeda, Palmyra, Pelmira.

Paloma

From the Latin, 'dove', which is the symbol of peace. Best known for Picasso's daughter Paloma.
OTHER FORMS: Palometa, Palomita.

Pamela

From the Greek, 'honey' and 'all'. The name became popular in the 18th century due to Samuel Richardson's novel *Pamela* and is still current.
OTHER FORMS: Pam, Pamella, Pammie.

Pandora

From the Greek, 'gifted in everything'. In the legend Pandora was given a box which she was forbidden to open, but she did and let out all the evils into the world, and only hope was left.

Pansy

From the French, 'thought'. This is the name of a flower of the viola family which has beautiful velvety petals.

Parvati
From the Sanskrit, 'of the mountain', this name refers to Shiva's wife.

Pascale
From the French, 'Easter', also known outside France.
OTHER FORMS: Paschal, Pasquale.

Patience
From the Latin, 'to suffer', this is one of the virtues which became given names under the Puritans.
SHORT FORMS: Patia, Pattie.

Patricia
The female form of Patrick, which comes from the Latin, 'nobleman'. First used in Scotland, it became fashionable in Victorian times.
SHORT FORMS: Pat, Patti, Tricia, Trish.

Patsy
A short form of Patricia.

Patti(e)
A short form of Patricia.

Patty
A short form of Patricia.

Paula
A female form of Paul. The name of a 4th-century Roman saint whose name spread from the Middle East where she founded several convents.
SHORT FORMS: Pol, Polly.

Paulette
French form of Paula.

Paulina
A Latin form of Paula.

Pauline
A Latin form of Paula.

Payal
An Indian name which means 'anklet'.
OTHER FORM: Paayal.

Peace
From the Latin, 'peace, tranquillity'.

Pearl
From the precious stone which is formed inside an oyster. It also has a derivation in a Yiddish word. Sometimes used as a pet form of Margaret, which comes from the Greek, 'pearl'.

Peg
A pet name for Margaret.
OTHER FORM: Peggy.

Pegeen
An Anglicized form of the Gaelic for Peg.

Pelagia
From the Greek, 'sea' or 'mermaid'.
There were several saints of this name.

Penelope
From the Greek, 'weaver'. The faithful
wife of mythical Greek hero Odysseus,
who waited for him for ten years.
SHORT FORMS: Pen, Pennie, Penny.

Peninah
From the Hebrew, 'coral' or 'pearl', this
is a biblical name.
OTHER FORMS: Penina, Peninna.

Peony
From the Greek, 'hymn of thanksgiving'.
The name of a flower with large pink,
red or white blossoms.
OTHER FORM: Paeony.

Perdita
From the Latin, 'lost', the name was
invented by Shakespeare for the heroine
of *The Winter's Tale*.
SHORT FORMS: Perdie, Perdy.

Pernille
The female form of the Scandinavian
version of Peter.

Persephone
The Greek mythical goddess of the
underworld.
OTHER FORM: Proserpina.

Peta
A modern female form of Peter.

Petal
From the petal of a flower, this is also a
term of endearment.

Petra
A female form of Peter, from the Latin,
'rock'. Best known for the dog in the
children's TV series Blue Peter.

Petrina
A modern female form of Peter.

Petronella
From the Latin family name Petronius.
SHORT FORM: Petronel.

Petronilla
An early martyr of this name was
believed to be the daughter of St Peter.

Petula
Possibly from the Latin, 'to ask', best
known from the singer Petula Clark.

Petunia

A flower name from the spring-flowering bedding plant.

Phebe

A variation of Phoebe.

Phedra

From the Greek, 'bright one'. She was the daughter of King Minos of Crete.
OTHER FORMS: Phaedra, Phaidra, Phedre.

Philippa

From the Greek, 'lover of horses', this is the female form of Philip.
OTHER FORMS: Philipa, Phillippa.

Philippine

A rare female form of Philip.

Phillida

A variation of Phyllis.
OTHER FORM: Phyllida.

Phillis

A variation of Phyllis.

Philomena

From the Greek, 'loving' and 'strength', it was wrongly thought to be a saint's name and was popular in the 19th century.
OTHER FORM: Filomena.

Phoebe

The female form of the Greek Phoebus, god of the sun. Used by Shakespeare, it was popular in Victorian times.
OTHER FORM: Phebe.

Phyllis

From the Greek, 'foliage'. A mythical girl who pined away from love and was turned into an almond tree.
SHORT FORMS: Phyl, Phyllie.

Pia

From the Latin, 'faithful', it is more usual in Italy.

Pilar

A Spanish name in honour of a vision of the Virgin Mary standing on a pillar.

Pippa

A short form of Philippa, used in its own right.

Polly

A short form of Mary or of Paula often used as a given name.
SHORT FORM: Poll.

Pooja

An Indian name meaning 'worship'.
OTHER FORM: Puja.

Poojita

An Indian name associated with the full moon.

Poppy

The name of the wild and cultivated flower, usually bearing red blooms.

Portia

From the Latin family name meaning 'pig'. It was the name of Shakespeare's heroine in *The Merchant of Venice*.
OTHER FORM: Porsha.

Posy

A pet name for Josephine.

Primrose

From the spring flower whose name means 'first rose' in Latin.

Primula

A spring flower.

Prisca

A variation of Priscilla.

Priscilla

From the Latin, 'ancient, antique', this name was popular with the Puritans in the 17th century and again in the late 19th century.
SHORT FORMS: Pris, Prissy, Cilla.

Priyal

From the Sanskrit, 'beloved'.
OTHER FORMS: Priyam, Priyanka, Priyasha.

Prudence

From the Latin, 'good sense'. One of the virtues, which were used as first names by the Puritans.
SHORT FORMS: Pru, Prue.

Prunella

From the Latin, 'little plum', it is the name of a bird and also a wild flower. Best known through the actress Prunella Scales.
SHORT FORMS: Pru, Prue.

Psyche

From the Greek, 'soul' or 'butterfly'. The mythical nymph Psyche was loved by Eros and was finally united with him on Mount Olympus.

Puja

A variation of Pooja.

Punam

A variation of Poonam.

Punita

An Indian name meaning pure.

P ~ Boys

Pablo
Spanish form of Paul.

Paddy
An Irish pet form of Patrick, sometimes used as the generic term for an Irishman.

Padma
From the Sanskrit, 'lotus', more often a girls' name denoting the goddess Lakshmi.
OTHER FORM: Padman.

Padraig
Irish Gaelic form of Patrick.

Painton
From the Latin, 'country town', this name was introduced into England by the Normans.
SHORT FORMS: Payne, Pyne.

Pan
From the Greek, 'all'. He was the god of fertility for animals.

Pancho
A Spanish name from the Latin, 'feather'.
OTHER FORM: Panchito.

Paolo
Italian form of Paul.

Paris
The son of the legendary king of Troy, whose abduction of Helen started the Trojan War.

Parker
The traditional name for the medieval keeper of a game park.
OTHER FORMS: Parke, Parkman.

Parry
From the Welsh, 'son of Harry'.

Parson
From the Latin, 'person of the church'.

Pascal
From the French, 'Easter', it is also used in the English-speaking world.
OTHER FORMS: Pasco, Pasqual.

Pat

A short form of Patrick.

Patrick

From the Latin, 'patrician, nobleman'. St Patrick is the patron saint of Ireland, where he converted the Irish to Christianity.

SHORT FORMS: Paddy, Pat, Rick.

Paul

From the Roman family name Paulus meaning 'small'. St Paul with St Peter was the co-founder of the Christian church and his name has been borne by many popes.

OTHER FORMS: Paulie, Paulinus, Pol, Powel.

Paxton

From the Latin, 'peace' and 'town'.

Pelham

From the Latin, 'skin, pelt' and 'village'. The Pelham family were dukes of Newcastle.

Penn

From the surname, it may have referred to someone who lived near a sheep pen. More usual in the US where Sir William Penn founded Pennsylvania.

OTHER FORMS: Pennie, Penny.

Pepin

From the Old German, 'petitioner'. Pepin the Short was King of the Franks and father of Charlemagne.

OTHER FORMS: Peppi, Peppie, Peppy.

Pepper

From the Sanskrit, 'berry'. The dried berries of the pepper vine are used to spice food.

Perce

A short form of Percival or Percy.

Perceval

From the surname which comes from Percheval, in Normandy.

Percival

The name of one of the legendary Knights of the Round Table who caught sight of the Holy Grail.

SHORT FORMS: Perce, Percy.

Percy

From the aristocratic surname of the Percy family, who were descended from William de Perci, one of William the Conqueror's knights. The poet Shelley bore the name and made it known in the 19th century.

Peregrine

From the Latin, 'traveller' and so 'pilgrim'. The 7th-century St Peregrine was a hermit in Italy.

SHORT FORM: Perry.

Perry

From the surname, which originated from someone who lived by a pear tree. The American singer Perry Como made the name known in the 20th century.

Peter

From the Greek, 'rock'. St Peter was the leading Apostle in the Bible and the first Bishop of Rome. Inumerable churches are dedicated to him.

OTHER FORMS: Pedro, Perkin, Pete, Pietro.

Phelim

The Irish form of Felix, meaning 'happy'.

Philip

From the Greek, 'lover of horses'. Philip was one of the Apostles in the Bible and it has been the name of several Spanish kings.

SHORT FORMS: Flip, Phil, Pip.

Phillip

A variation of Philip and a transferred surname, which is usually spelt Phillips.

Phineas

The name of two minor characters in the Bible. Best known for the Jules Verne character, Phineas Fogg, who circumnavigated the globe in 80 days.

OTHER FORMS: Phinhas, Finny.

Pierce

The English and Irish form of Piers, it may also be a transferred surname.

Piers

A French form of Peter.

Pip

A short form of Philip.

Pius

From the Latin, 'devout, respectful', this has been the name of 12 popes.

Pomeroy

From the French, 'apple', therefore a gardener who looks after orchards. A transferred surname.

Pompey

From the Latin, 'young vine shoot'. Pompey was a great Roman general, and this is also the name sailors give to Portsmouth.

OTHER FORM: Pompeo.

Poojan

An Indian name meaning 'worship'.

Poojit

An Indian name meaning 'worshipped'.

Porter

From the French, 'to carry', this was the name given to someone who guarded the gate.

Pratik

An Indian name meaning 'a symbol'.

Preston

From the Old English, 'priest' and 'town', this is the name of a town in Lancashire.

Prince

From the Latin, 'the principal', this name for the son of a king is used as a first name in the US in the same way as Duke or Earl.

Prior

From the Latin, 'the first', this is a transferred surname.

Priya

An Indian name meaning 'beloved'.

Prospero

From the Latin, 'fortunate, prosperous'. The name of the exiled duke with magical powers in Shakespeare's *The Tempest*.

Pryderi

A traditional name from the Welsh 'caring for'.

Puja

A variation of Pooja.
OTHER FORM: Pujan.

Pujit

A variation of Poojit.

Punam

A variation of Poonam.

Punit

An Indian name meaning 'pure'.

Q ~ Girls

Queenie
From the Old English, 'queen', this was a nickname given to girls named after Queen Victoria. Originally it was a pet name for Regina, the Latin for queen, and in the Middle Ages it referred to the Virgin Mary, as Queen of Heaven.

OTHER FORMS: Queena, Quenie.

Querida
Spanish for 'loved one' or 'darling'.

Quinta
From the Latin, 'fifth', traditionally given to the fifth child who was a girl. It can also refer to the date on which she was born.

OTHER FORMS: Quintilla, Quintina.

Q ~ Boys

Qadim
From the Arabic, 'ancient'.

Qasim
From the Arabic, 'one who distributes'. This is the name of one of the sons of the Propher Muhammad.

Quentin
The French form of the name from the Latin, 'fifth'. It was the name of a 3rd-century saint and became known through the Walter Scott novel *Quentin Durward*.

Quincy
The name derived from the surname of a French family who came from Normandy. John Quincy Adams was President of the United States in the 18th century and there is also a place in Massachusetts with the name.
OTHER FORM: Quincey.

Quinn
From the Irish surname meaning 'descended from Conn'. It is also a short form of Quincy or Quinton.

Quintin
A variation of Quentin.

Quinton
From the surname, which derives from the Old English, 'queen' and 'town'.

R ~ Girls

Rabia
From the Arabic, 'fragrant breeze' or 'garden'.

Rachael
A variation of Rachel.

Rachel
From the Hebrew, 'ewe, female sheep' meaning someone who is innocent as a lamb. In the Bible Rachel was the beautiful wife of Jacob and mother of Benjamin and Joseph.
SHORT FORMS: Rach, Rachie, Rae, Ray.

Rachelle
A variation of Rachel.

Radha
From the Sanskrit, 'success' this is the name of Krishna's preferred consort.
OTHER FORM: Radhika.

Rae
A short form of Rachel, also used in its own right, particularly in Australia.

Raelene
A mainly Australian form of Rae.

Raheel
An Arabic name, a variation of Rahil.
OTHER FORM: Raheela.

Rahil
An Arabic version of Rachel.

Rahima
A female form of Rahim, from the Arabic, 'compassionate'.
OTHER FORMS: Rahima, Raheema(h).

Rainbow
A word taken from nature by parents during the flower power movement in the 1960s.

Raine
From the Latin, 'authority' or the French 'queen'. Best known through Countess Raine Spencer, the stepmother of Diana, Princess of Wales.
OTHER FORMS: Raina, Rana, Rayne.

Raisa

A Russian name meaning 'paradise'. It became known because of the wife of the Russian President Gorbachev.
OTHER FORM: Raissa.

Rajani

From the Sanskrit, 'the dark one'. This is one of the names of the Hindu goddess Shiva.

Rajni

From the Sanskrit, 'queen' and also a short form of Rajani.

Ramona

From the German, 'wise protector' and a female form of Raymond.

Rana

From the Arabic, 'beautiful object'.

Randa

A female form of Randall or Randolph.

Randy

A pet form of Miranda.
OTHER FORMS: Randi, Randie.

Rani

A variation of Rajni.

Rapa

From the Hawaiian, 'moonbeam'.

Raphaela

The Italian female form of Raphael.

Raquel

The Spanish form of Rachel. Best known because of the filmstar Raquel Welch.

Raven

The name of the large glossy black bird, this is used mainly by Afro-American parents, probably due to the colour of the bird.

Ravenna

From the name of the town in Italy and also as an elaboration of Raven.

Ray

The female short form of Raymond, used in its own right.
OTHER FORM: Raymonde.

Rayna

Possibly from the Yiddish, 'pure' and a variation of Raine.

Razina

From the Arabic, 'contented', this is a mainly Muslim name.

Rebecca

This is a biblical name. In its Hebrew form, Rebekah, she was Isaac's lovely wife. An enduringly popular name amongst all faiths.
SHORT FORMS: Becca, Becky.

Rebekka

A variation of Rebecca.

Reenie

An Anglicized form of Renée and also short for Irene or Maureen.

Regan

Taken from an Irish surname, possibly connected with the Gaelic, 'queen'. The name was used by Shakespeare for one of the daughters in *King Lear.*

Regina

From the Latin, 'queen', this was the name of an early French saint.
SHORT FORMS: Gina, Reggie, Regine.

Reiko

From the Japanese, 'gratitude'.

Reine

French form of Regina.

Renée

From the Latin, 'reborn', the French name is also used in Britain without the accent.

Renata

From the Latin, 'born again', used more often in continental Europe.

Renie

A short form of Irene.

Reshma

An Indian name which means 'silken'.

Rexana

The female form of Rex.

Rhea

From the Greek, 'protectress'. She was the mother of the mythical founders of Rome.

Rhiannon

A Welsh name meaning 'great queen'. She was probably a Celtic goddess, but the name has only been used in the 20th century.
OTHER FORM: Rhianna.

Rhoda

From the Greek, 'rose', which also was the derivation of the shrub rhododendron.

Rhona

From the name of a Scottish island and a variation of Rona.

Rhonda

From the Celtic, 'powerful river', this is the name of a region in Wales.
OTHER FORMS: Rhondda, Ronda.

Rhonwen

From the Welsh, 'fair lance'.

Ria

From the Spanish, 'small river' and also a short form of Maria.

Riannon

A variation of Rhiannon.
OTHER FORM: Rianna.

Ricarda

A female form of Richard.

Richelle

A modern female form of Richard.

Richenda

A modern female form of Richard.

Rickma

From the Hebrew, 'woven'.

Rilla

From the German, 'small stream, brook'.

Rina

A short form of Carina or Katerina.

Riona

A short form of Catriona.

Rita

A short form of Margarita, but more usual as a name in its own right. It is also an Indian name meaning 'brave, strong'.

Riva

From the French, 'river bank'.

Roberta

A female form of Robert.

Robina

A female form of Robin.

Robyn

A female form of Robin.

Rochelle

From the French, 'little rock', implying someone who is reliable.

Roda

A variation of Rhoda.

Rohan

From the Sanskrit, possibly meaning 'sandalwood'. Another name for Adam's Peak, Sri Lanka's sacred mountain, which has the imprint of a foot on its summit.

Roisin

The Irish pet form of the Gaelic, which means 'little rose'.

Rolanda

The female form of Roland.

Romelda

From the German, 'warrior maiden'.
OTHER FORM: Romilda.

Romey

A short form of Rosemary.
OTHER FORM: Romy.

Romola

From the Latin, 'lady of Rome'.

Rona

A variation of Rhona and a short form of Rhonwen.

Ronat

The female form of Ronan.

Ronnie

A short form of Veronica.

Ros

A short form of Rosalind and Rosamund.

Rosa

A Latin variation of Rose.

Rosabel

From the Latin, 'beautiful rose'.
OTHER FORM: Rosabella.

Rosalba

From the Latin, 'white rose'.

Rosaleen

A Irish form of Roisin.

Rosalia

Taken from a Roman festival when tombs were decorated with garlands of roses. Rosalia was a 12th-century saint who is the patron of Palermo in Sicily.

Rosalie

The French form of Rosalia.

Rosalind

From the Spanish, 'pretty rose', the name was used for the heroine in Shakespeare's *As You Like It*.
SHORT FORMS: Ros, Roz.

Rosaline

A variation of Rosalind.

Rosalyn

A medieval form of Rosalind.
OTHER FORMS: Rosalynne, Roslyn.

Rosamund

From the Latin, 'rose of the world', this name was brought to England by the Normans.
OTHER FORMS: Rosamond, Roz.

Rosanna

A combination name of Rose and Anna.
OTHER FORM: Rosanne.

Rose

From the flower name which is often denoted as a symbol for the Virgin Mary. This is the most popular of all the flower names.
SHORT FORMS: Rosie, Rosy.

Roseanne

A combination of the name Rose and Anne.

Rosebud

A pet name for Rose, sometimes used as a first name.

Roselle

A modern combination of Rose and 'elle'.

Rosemary

From the Latin, 'sea dew', this is the name of an aromatic herb used in cookery.
OTHER FORMS: Rosemarie, Romey, Romy.

Rosetta

From the Latin, 'little rose'.

Rosheen

The Anglicized form of the Irish Roisin.

Rosina

A variation of Rose.

Rosita

A diminutive of Rose.

Roshni

From the Persian, 'famous' or 'shining', this is mainly a Muslim name.

Rosie

A pet form of Rose or Rosemary.
OTHER FORM: Rosy.

Roslyn

A variation of Rosalind.

Rowan

From the name of the tree which has bright red berries.
OTHER FORM: Rowanne.

Rowena

A Latin form of an old Saxon name, borne by the daughter of Hengist. Sir Walter Scott used the name in his novel *Ivanhoe*.

OTHER FORM: Rowina.

Roxana

A variation of Roxane.

Roxane

From the Persian, 'dawn' or 'bright light'. It was the name of a beautiful courtesan in a novel by Daniel Defoe.

OTHER FORMS: Roxanna, Roxanne.

Roxy

A short form of Roxane.

Roz

A short form of Rosalind or Rosamund.

Rube

A short form of Ruby.

Ruby

From the Latin, 'red', this is taken from the name of a gemstone.

Rula

From the Latin, 'pattern' or 'model'. This name became known through the actress Rula Lenska.

Rumer

An English gypsy name possibly derived from Romany. The name of the novelist Rumer Godden.

Runa

From the Norse, 'to flow'.

Rupli

From the Sanskrit, 'beautiful', this is the female form of Rupak.

Rusty

A nickname for someone with reddish-brown hair.

Ruth

A biblical name for the daughter-in-law of Naomi, who gave her name to one of the books in the New Testament. It is also connected with the meaning 'sorrow' or 'pity'.

OTHER FORM: Ruthie.

R ~ Boys

Rab
A Scottish short form of Robert.
OTHER FORM: Rabbie.

Radhakrishna
The name of the Indian god, Krishna, added to his beloved Radha, to symbolise the dual nature of the supreme god.

Rafe
An old form of Ralph, used before the 'l' started to be pronounced in the 20th century.

Rafferty
From the Gaelic, 'rich and prosperous', this transferred surname is used mainly in the US.

Raheem
A variation of Rahim.

Rahim
From the Arabic, 'compassionate' or 'merciful', this is one of Allah's qualities.

Rai
A short form of Raymond.

Rainier
A French name derived from the Latin, 'kingly'. Made well known through Prince Rainier of Monaco, who married the filmstar Grace Kelly.

Raja
From the Sanskrit, 'king' and the Arabic 'hope'.
SHORT FORM: Raj.

Rajan
From the Sanskrit, 'king'.

Rajendra
From the Sanskrit, 'mighty king'.

Rajesh
From the Sanskrit, 'ruler of kings'.

Rajnish
From the Sanskrit, 'ruler of the night', which refers to the moon.
OTHER FORM: Rajneesh.

Raleigh

From the Old English, 'roe deer'. Sir Walter Raleigh was the Elizabethan courtier and explorer.

OTHER FORMS: Rawley, Rawly.

Ralf

A variation of Ralph.

Ralph

From the Old English, 'advice' and 'wolf'. The original name Radulf was used before the Norman Conquest. Ralf or Rafe were used until the 'ph' ending appeared in the 18th century.

OTHER FORMS: Raaf, Rauf.

Rama

From the Sanskrit, 'pleasing'. Ramachandra is an incarnation of Vishnu and is worshipped in India.

Ramsay

From the Old English, 'sheep' and 'island'. This is a transferred use of the Scottish surname, from an English place name. Ramsay Macdonald was the first Labour Prime Minister in Britain.

OTHER FORM: Ramsey.

Ran

A short form of Ranald, Randall and Randolf.

Ranald

The Anglicized form of the Gaelic name Raghnall, meaning 'advice' and 'ruler'.

Randall

A variation of Randolph.

Randolph

From the Old English name meaning 'shield' and 'wolf'.

SHORT FORMS: Dolph, Rand, Randi.

Randy

A short form of Andrew or Randall, in the US this is used as a name in its own right.

Ranulf

The name was introduced into Scotland in the Middle Ages by settlers from Scandinavia. It is also a variation of Randolph.

Raoul

The French form of Ralph.

Raphael

From the Hebrew, 'healed by God', this is the name of one of the Archangels in the Bible. The Italian Renaissance painter Raffaelo Santi was known as Raphael.

OTHER FORMS: Rafael, Rafaello, Rafi.

Raqib
From the Arabic for a supervisor of spiritual things.

Rashad
From the Arabic, 'good sense' or 'integrity'.

Rashid
From the Arabic, 'rightly guided'.

Rastus
A short form of Erastus, the name of a Greek from Corinth who was converted to Christianity by St Paul.

Rauf
A variation of Ralph.

Raul
The Spanish form of Ralph.

Raven
The name of the black bird, which has made it popular with Afro-Americans. More usual as a girl's name.

Ravi
From the Sanskrit, 'sun', this is the Indian name for the god of the sun.

Ravindra
From the Sanskrit, 'mightiest of suns'.

Ray
A short form of Raymond, also used as a given name.

Raymond
From the Old English, 'advice' and 'protection'. The name was popular during the Crusades due to two saints who bore the name.
SHORT FORMS: Rai, Ray.

Read
A transferred surname, from the Old English, 'red' or 'reeds'.
OTHER FORM: Reid.

Redmond
An Irish form of Raymond.

Reece
A variation of Rhys.

Reeves
From the Old English, 'steward', this is one of the names that derive from occupations.

Reg
A short form of Reginald.
OTHER FORMS: Reggie, Reggy.

Reginald

From the Old English, 'powerful warrior'. The Normans derived the name from the Latin Reginaldus, influenced by the Latin word for 'queen'.

SHORT FORMS: Reg, Reggie, Rex.

Reid

A variation of Read.

Reinald

A French form of Reginald.

Reith

From the Scottish surname, possibly connected with the Gaelic, 'grace'.

Remus

From the Latin, 'swift oarsman'. This was the name of one of the founders of Rome.

OTHER FORMS: Remer, Remy

René

A French name from the Latin, 'reborn'. The Latin form Renatus was used by the 17th-century Puritans.

Reuben

From the Hebrew, 'behold a son'. In the Bible this is one of the 12 sons of Jacob, who founded one of the tribes of Israel.

OTHER FORM: Ruben.

Rex

From the Latin, 'king' or 'ruler', this has only been used as a first name since the 19th century.

Reynard

From the Old German, 'advice' and 'strong'. It also has associations with the French for 'fox'.

Reynaud

A French form of Reginald.

Reynold

From the Old French name Reinald or Reynaud.

Rhett

From the Anglicized Dutch surname, used in the southern US. Best known for the seductive character, Rhett Butler, in the film and novel *Gone with the Wind*.

Rhodri

From the Welsh, 'crowned ruler'.

Rydderch

From the Welsh, 'reddish-brown'.

Rhys

From the Welsh, 'rashness'. The name of a famous prince who turned the Normans back from the Welsh borders.
OTHER FORMS: Reece, Reese.

Rian

A variation of Ryan.

Ricardo

The Italian and Spanish form of Richard.

Rich

A short form of Richard and also a name in its own right in medieval times.
OTHER FORM: Richie.

Richard

From the Old German, 'power' and 'brave'. This has been the name of three English kings and of the 13th-century St Richard of Chichester.
SHORT FORMS: Diccon, Dick(y), Rick(y), Rich, Rico.

Rickie

A short form of Richard.
OTHER FORM: Ricky.

Rider

From the Anglo-Saxon, 'knight, horse-rider'.
OTHER FORM: Ryder.

Ridley

From the surname meaning 'reeds' and 'clearing' in Old English. The Puritans used the name in honour of Bishop Ridley who was burnt at the stake for being a Protestant.

Riley

From the Old English, 'rye meadow', this comes from the surname and from English place names.
OTHER FORMS: Reilly, Ryley.

Riordan

From the Gaelic, 'royal poet', this is a mainly Irish name.
OTHER FORM: Rearden.

Rishi

An Indian name meaning 'wise man'.

Roald

From the German, 'famous ruler', is known through the writer Roald Dahl.

Robert

From the Old German, 'bright' and 'famous'. Brought to England by the Normans, it has been consistently used since then. King Robert the Bruce made the name popular in Scotland.
SHORT FORMS: Bob, Bobbie, Rab, Rabbie, Rob, Robbie.

Robin

Originally a French variation of Robert. Robin Hood was the legendary outlaw, and Christopher Robin the hero of A. A. Milne's Winnie the Pooh stories.

SHORT FORM: Rob.

Rochester

From the Old English, 'rock' and 'fortress'. A transferred surname and the name of a town in England.

Short forms: Chester, Rock, Rocky.

Rocky

A recent coinage in the US. It was made known by the boxer Rocky Marciano.

Rod

A short form of Roderick and Rodney. Known through the name of several American filmstars including Rod Stewart.

OTHER FORM: Roddy.

Roderick

From the Old German, 'famous ruler', it is an Anglicized form of the Spanish name Rodrigo.

SHORT FORMS: Rod, Roddy.

Rodge

A short form of Roger.

Rodger

A variation of Roger.

Rodney

From the Old English, 'island of reeds'. Used as a first name in the 18th century, from the surname of Admiral Lord Rodney.

SHORT FORMS: Rod, Roddy.

Roger

From Old German and Old English variations of names meaning 'famous spearman'. The diminutive, Hodge, became a name for a peasant labourer and so was out of fashion for a while.

SHORT FORMS: Rog, Roggie.

Rohan

From the Sanskrit, 'ascending', it is also taken to mean 'healing'.

Roland

From the Old German, 'fame' and land'. The old French Song of Roland told of the exploits of this famous warrior and his great friendship with Oliver.

SHORT FORMS: Roly, Rowley.

Rolf

From the Old German, 'fame' and 'wolf', the name was imported from Germany in the 19th century.
OTHER FORMS: Rolph, Roulf.

Rollo

A variation of Roland.

Roly

A short form of Roland.

Romeo

From the Latin, 'Roman citizen'. A romantic name associated with Shakespeare's hero of Romeo and Juliet.

Romney

From the Celtic, 'curving river'.

Ronak

From the Sanskrit, 'embellisment'.

Ronald

From an old Norse name, this is a Scottish form of Reginald, now used in other places as well.
SHORT FORMS: Ron, Ronnie.

Ronan

From the Gaelic, 'little seal'. The name of several early saints, one of whom was a missionary in Cornwall.

Roper

From the German, 'rope-maker'.

Rory

From the Gaelic, 'red-haired'. Rory O'Connor was a famous king in Ireland.
OTHER FORM: Rorie.

Roscoe

From the surname with the Old Norse meaning of 'deer wood'.

Roshan

From the Persian, 'shining' or 'splendid'.

Ross

The name of a clan in Scotland, from the Gaelic, 'peninsular'.
OTHER FORMS: Rossie, Rossy, Royce.

Rowan

From the Gaelic, 'little red one' it is associated with the rowan tree, which had bright red berries. The name was borne by an early Irish saint.
OTHER FORMS: Rowie, Rowen, Rowney.

Rowland

From the Old English, 'rugged land' and also a variation of Roland.

Roy

From the Gaelic, 'red'. Rob Roy was the 18th-century red-haired Highlander who helped the poor at the expense of the rich.

Royle

From the place name meaning 'rye' and 'hill' in Old English.

Ruadhan

From the Irish, 'little red one'.

Ruari

An Irish Gaelic name meaning 'red-haired'.

OTHER FORMS: Ruairi, Ruaridh.

Ruben

A variation of Reuben.

Rudolph

From the Old German, 'famous wolf'. King Rudolph I was a Holy Roman Emperor in the 13th century.

OTHER FORMS: Rudi, Rudolf, Rudy.

Rufus

From the Latin, 'red-haired' . William Rufus became King William II.

Rupad

From the Sanskrit, 'beautiful'.

OTHER FORM: Rupesh.

Rupchand

From the Sanskrit, 'as beautiful as the moon'.

Rupert

As with Robert this comes from the Old German, 'bright' and 'fame'. And it is the English form of the German Rupprecht. The dashing Prince Rupert of the Rhine took the name to England during the Civil War.

SHORT FORM: Rupe.

Russ

A short form of Russell, now used in its own right.

Russell

From the surname, derived from the French word for 'red'. The fashion for aristocratic surnames used as first names started in the 19th century.

OTHER FORMS: Russ, Russel.

Rusty

A nickname for someone with red hair.

Ryan

From the Gaelic, 'little king'. Best known through the filmstar Ryan O'Neal.

OTHER FORM: Rian.

S ~ Girls

Sabah
From the Arabic, 'morning', this is the name of a well-known Lebanese singer.

Sabina
From the Latin, 'a woman of the Sabines', who were an old Italian race that was conquered by the Romans. St Sabina was an early Roman martyr.
OTHER FORM: Savina.

Sabine
The French form of Sabina.

Sabra
From the Hebrew, 'thorny cactus'. The name given to native-born Israelis to denote a prickly exterior, but gentle nature.
OTHER FORM: Zabra.

Sabrina
This was the ancient name for the River Severn before the Romans conquered Britain, from which came the name of the legendary river-sprite.

Sacha
From the Greek, 'helpmate'. Also a Russian short form of Alexander, which is sometimes used as a girl's name.

Sadie
A pet form of Sarah, but also used in its own right.

Saffron
This name, taken from the yellow-coloured spice which derives from the crocus flower, was particularly popular in the 1960s.
SHORT FORM: Saffie.

Sahila
An Indian name meaning 'beloved'.

Sakura
From the Japanese, 'cherry blossom'.

Sal
A short form of Sally.

Salah
From the Arabic, 'goodness', this name is used by Muslims.

Salima
From the Arabic, 'safe, unharmed'.

Salina
From the Latin, 'salt water'.
OTHER FORM: Salena.

Sally
A pet form of Sarah, this can be combined with other names such as Ann.
OTHER FORMS: Sal, Sallie.

Salome
Greek, from the original Aramaic, 'peace', of which another form is the Hebrew 'shalom'. This was the name of the princess who danced the Dance of the Seven Veils in the Bible.
OTHER FORMS: Saloma, Salomi.

Salvia
From the Latin for 'sage herb'. A flower name taken from the red or blue wild or garden plant.

Sam
A short form of Samantha.

Samantha
From the Aramaic, 'a listener'.
OTHER FORMS: Sam, Sammy.

Samimah
From the Arabic, 'sincere'.
OTHER FORM: Sameema, Sameemah.

Samara
From the Hebrew, 'guarded by God'.

Samira
From the Arabic, 'companion in night talk'.
OTHER FORMS: Sameera(h), Samirah.

Samuela
A female form of Samuel.

Sana
From the Arabic, 'brilliance' or 'radiance'.

Sancha
A Spanish name from the Latin, 'sacred'. It has been known in Britain since the 13th century, when, as Sanchia, it was brought over by the daughter of a provencal count.
OTHER FORM: Sanchia.

Sandip
An Indian name meaning 'beautiful'.

Sandra

A short form of the Italian female form of Alexander, used in its own right.
OTHER FORMS: Sandie, Sandy, Sondra, Zandra.

Saniyya

From the Arabic, 'illustrious'.

Sandy

A short form of Sandra.

Santa

From the Latin, 'holy' or 'pure'.

Sapphire

The name of a jewel of different colours but usually associated with deep blue.
OTHER FORMS: Safir, Sapphira.

Sappho

The name of a 6th-century Greek poet, noted for her love for other women.

Sara

The Greek form of Sarah.

Sarah

From the Hebrew, 'princess' this is one of the most enduring of biblical names. Sarah was the wife of Abraham and mother of Isaac.
OTHER FORMS: Sadie, Sal, Sara.

Saraid

From the Irish, 'excellent'.

Sarika

An Indian name meaning 'black cuckoo'.

Sarita

A variation of Sarah.

Sasha

The English spelling of the short form of Alessandra.

Saskia

Possibly derived from 'Saxon'. This was the name of Rembrandt's wife, whose portraits first introduced it to England from Holland.

Satin

From the name of the smooth, silky fabric. Originally a French word derived from the Arabic.

Savannah

From the names of cities in the southern US and the river of the same name.

Scarlett
From the Old French, 'vivid red cloth'. Best known through the character in the romantic novel and film *Gone with the Wind*.
OTHER FORM: Scarlet.

Sean
The Irish form of John, but also used for girls.

Sejal
An Indian name meaning 'river' or 'water'.

Selda
From the Old English, 'rare'.
OTHER FORM: Zelda.

Selena
A variation of Selene.

Selene
From the Greek, 'moon'. Another name for Artemis, mythical goddess of the moon.

Selima
Possibly from the Arabic, 'peaceful', the name was recorded as the name of Horace Walpole's cat in the 18th century.

Selina
Probably a variation of Selena or of the French Céline.
OTHER FORM: Celina.

Selma
From the Celtic, 'fair', the name is found in northern Europe and in the US.

Semele
From the Latin, 'the single one'.

Semiramis
The mythical Assyrian who married King Ninus and founded Babylon.

Septima
From the Latin, 'seventh'. Originally given to the seventh child but it can be used for a child born in the seventh month or on the seventh day.

Seraphina
From the Hebrew, 'to burn'. In the Bible the seraphs were three-winged angels.
OTHER FORMS: Serafina, Serafine, Seraphine.

Serena
From the Latin, 'calm, serene'.
OTHER FORM: Sirena.

Shaina
From the Hebrew, 'beautiful'.

Shakira
From the Arabic, 'thankful'.
OTHER FORM: Shaira.

Shalene
A variation of Charlene.

Shan
A short form of Shantelle.

Shana
A variation of Sian.

Shanae
An Afro-American name, of recent invention.
OTHER FORMS: Shanay, Shanaye.

Shani
A pet form of Sian.

Shanice
An Afro-American combination of Shan and Janice.

Shaniqua
A blend of Shan and Monique or Monica, popular among Afro-Americans.
OTHER FORM: Shanika.

Shannah
A short form of the Hebrew variation of Susanna.

Shannelle
A variation of Chanel.
OTHER FORM: Shanel.

Shannon
From the name of the Irish river.

Shantelle
A variation of Chantal or Chantelle.

Shari
From Sari, the Hungarian form of Sara. Also a pet form of Sharon.

Sharifa
From the Arabic, 'eminent' or 'honourable'. The title given to descendants of the Prophet Muhammad.

Sharissa
A modern blend of Sharon with Clarissa or Nerissa.

Sharlene
A variation of Charlene.

Sharlott
A variation of Charlotte.

Sharmaine

A variation of Charmaine.

Sharon

Taken from the Song of Solomon in the Bible, which tells of the rose of Sharon. Also the name of a yellow-flowered shrub.

OTHER FORMS: Shari, Sharron.

Sharona

A variation of Sharon.

Shawna

A female variation of Sean.

Shayla

An American variation of Sheila.

Shea

From the Gaelic surname, possibly meaning 'fine'.

Sheba

A short form of Bathsheba. Also from the biblical Queen of Sheba.

Sheela

A variation of Sheila.

Sheena

An Anglicized form of Sine, the Gaelic form of Jane.

Sheila

From the Irish form of Cecilia, Sile.

OTHER FORMS: Sheela, Shiela.

Shelagh

A variation of Sheila.

Shelby

From the mainly American surname. Best known from a character in the film *Steel Magnolias*.

Shelley

A variation of Shirley or a pet form of Michelle and Rachel.

Sheridan

From the surname, possibly associated with the Gaelic, 'to seek'. More usual as a name for boys.

Sherie

A variation of Cherie.

OTHER FORM: Sheree.

Sherry

The Anglicized name of the Spanish town which is the centre of the sherry wine-growing district. Also a variation of Cherie.

Sheryl

A variation of Cheryl
OTHER FORM: Sheril.

Shevaun

A variation of Siobhan.

Shiela

A variation of Sheila.

Shirley

From the Old English, 'shire' and
'meadow'. Best known from one of
Charlotte Brontë's novels and the film
Shirley Valentine.

Shona

The female form of the Irish name Sean.
OTHER FORM: Shuna.

Shula

A short form of Shulamit. Popular due
to the radio serial *The Archers*.

Shulamit

From the Hebrew, 'peacefulness'.

Shyama

From the Sanskrit, 'dark', this is one of
the names of the Hindu goddess Durga.
OTHER FORMS: Shyamal(a), Shyamalenda,
Shyamari.

Shyann

From the native American Cheyenne
tribe, which is pronounced like this.

Sian

The Welsh for Jane.
OTHER FORMS: Shani, Siani.

Sibyl

A variation of Sibyl.
OTHER FORM: Sybilla.

Sidonia

From the Latin, 'woman from Sidon'.
OTHER FORMS: Sidney, Sidony.

Sidonie

The French form of Sidonia.

Sidra

From the Latin, 'star' or 'the heavens'.

Siena

A name taken from the beautiful Italian
town.

Sierra

From the Spanish, 'mountain range', this
is mainly used as a first name in the US.

Sigrid

From the Norse, 'victory' and 'fair'. The
female form of Siegfried.

Sile
The Gaelic form of Cecilia.

Silver
From the precious metal used for jewellery and currency.

Silvia
From the Latin, 'of the wood'. One of the names of the mother of Romulus and Remus, the founders of Rome.
SHORT FORM: Silvie.

Simone
The French female form of Simon.

Sindy
The American variation of Cindy. Best known for the Sindy doll.

Sine
The Irish Gaelic form of Jane.

Sinead
The Irish Gaelic form of Janet. Well known through the actress Sinead Cusack.

Siobhan
The Irish Gaelic form of Joan.

Sirena
From the Greek, 'temptress'. The sirens were mermaids who sang to entice sailors onto the rocks.

Sisley
A variation of Cecily or Cicely.

Sissy
A pet form of Cicely.
OTHER FORMS: Sis, Sissie.

Sita
From the Sanskrit, 'furrow', refering to the Hindu goddess of agriculture.
OTHER FORMS: Seeta, Seetha.

Sive
From the Irish for 'sweet'.

Skye
Taken from the name of the Scottish island.
OTHER FORM: Sky.

Slaney
From the Irish surname derived from the Gaelic, 'challenge'.

Sloane
From the surname and associated with the square in London, known for fashionable young women.

Sofia
A variation of Sophia.

Sofie
A variation of Sophie.

Solana
From the Spanish, 'sunshine'.

Solange
From the Old French, 'sole' and 'angel'.
A French name seldom found in
English-speaking countries.

Sonal
An Indian name which means 'golden'.

Sondra
A variation of Sandra.

Sonia
A variation of Sonya.

Sonja
A variation of Sonia and Sonya.

Sonya
A Russian pet form of Sophia.

Sophia
From the Greek, 'wisdom'. The name of
many Orthodox churches is Agia Sophia,
so it was taken as a girl's name in Greece.
OTHER FORM: Sofia.

Sophie
The Anglicized form of Sophia.
OTHER FORM: Sophy.

Sorcha
From the Gaelic, 'brightness', it is the
Irish form of Sarah.

Sorrel
From the name of the plant used for
salads and soups. Derived from the Old
French, 'sour'.

Spring
From the Old English, 'to leap up'. The
name of the season and a symbol of youth.

Sri
From the Sanskrit, 'light' or 'beauty' and
also used as a title. It is one of the names
of the Hindu goddess Lakshmi.
OTHER FORMS: Shree, Shri, Sree.

Stacey
Originally a short form of Anastasia,
now common in its own right.
SHORT FORM: Stace.

Star

Taken from the vocabulary word, this name implies fame and excellence.
OTHER FORM: Starr.

Steff

A short form of Stephanie.
OTHER FORM: Stef(f)ie.

Steffany

A variation of Stephanie.

Stella

From the Latin, 'star'. Stella Maris, 'star of the sea' is an established name for the Virgin Mary.

Steph

A short form of Stephanie.

Stephanie

From the Greek, 'crown' or 'garland', this is the female form of Stephen.
SHORT FORMS: Steph, Stephie.

Storm

From the Old English, 'tempestuous weather'. Best known for the novelist Storm Jameson.

Sue

A short form of Susan.

Sukey

A pet form of Susan.

Suki

A Japanese name meaning 'beloved'.

Sunila

The female form of Sunil.

Sunita

From the Sanskrit, probably meaning 'of good conduct'. The name of a princess of Bengal in an old epic poem.
OTHER FORM: Suniti.

Sunny

From the vocabulary word, implying a happy disposition.

Susan

The most common English form of Susanna.
SHORT FORMS: Su, Sue, Susie.

Susanna

The biblical form of the Hebrew name which means 'lily'.

Susannah

A variation of Susanna, this was used in the Middle Ages.
OTHER FORM: Suzanna.

Suzanne
French form of Susanna.

Suzette
French pet form of Suzanne and the name given to thin, sweet pancakes.

Swan
A name taken from the large, white or black aquatic birds. A symbol of elegance and grace.

Sybil
The classical Greek foretellers of the future.
OTHER FORMS: Sybilla, Sybille.

Sydel
From the Hebrew, 'that enchantress'.

Sydney
From the Latin name 'woman from Sidon'. The Australian city was named after Viscount Sydney and the name was given to girls in the 19th century.

Sylvana
A female form of Silvester, more used in Australia.

Sylvestra
A female form of Silvester.

Sylvia
A variation of Silvia.

Sylvie
A short form of Sylvia.

S ~ Boys

Sabin
From the name of an old Italian tribe conquered by the Romans.

Sacha
The Russian short form of Alexander.

Sacheverell
From a Norman baronial family name, meaning 'deer's leap'. Best known through the writer Sacheverell Sitwell.
SHORT FORM: Sachie.

Sagar
An Indian name which means 'ocean'.
OTHER FORMS: Saagar.

Sahil
An Indian name meaning 'guide'.

St John
A contraction of Saint John. This mainly Catholic first name has been in use since the middle of the 19th century. It is usually pronounced 'sin-jen'.

Sajan
An Indian name which means 'beloved'.

Sajjad
A name used by Muslims meaning 'prostrates', that is someone who lies full length to worship God.
OTHER FORM: Sajad.

Sakima
From a native American word meaning 'king'.

Saladin
From the Arabic, 'goodness of faith'. This was the name of the great 12th-century sultan who defeated the Crusaders and took Jerusalem.

Salah
From the Arabic, 'goodness' or 'righteousness'. A popular Muslim name.

Sale
From the Latin, 'salty'. The name infers someone who is the salt of the earth.

Salim

From the Arabic, 'perfect'.
OTHER FORM: Selim.

Salman

From the Arabic, 'safe' or 'unharmed'.
Best known for the author Salman
Rushdie.

Salvador

From the Latin, 'saved, unharmed'. This
was the name of the surrealist painter
Salvador Dali.
OTHER FORMS: Sal, Salvator.

Sammy

A pet form of Sam, from Samuel.

Sami

From the Arabic, 'exalted, high up'.

Samir

From the Arabic, 'entertainment'.
OTHER FORM: Sameer.

Samson

From the Hebrew, 'child of the sun'. In
the Bible he is the immensely strong
man, betrayed by Delilah, who single
handedly destroyed the temple of the
Philistines.
OTHER FORMS: Sam, Sammy, Sampson.

Samuel

From the Hebrew, 'heard by God'. A
biblical prophet and leader of the
Israelites who anointed Saul as their first
king.
SHORT FORMS: Sam, Sammie, Samy.

Sancho

Spanish for 'sincere, truthful'. It was the
name of Don Quixote's servant in the
17th-century story by Cervantes.
OTHER FORM: Sanche.

Sander

A short form of Alexander.

Sanford

From the Old English surname meaning
'sandy ford'.
OTHER FORM: Sandford.

Sanjay

From the Sanskrit, 'triumphant' . The
name of a narrator in the classic Hindu
epic poems. Known because of Sanjay
Ghandi, the son of a former Indian
prime minister, it is also the name of a
character in *East Enders*.

Sandy

A short form of Alexander.

Santiago

Spanish for St James and the name of a place in north-west Spain.

Sardis

From the Latin, 'carnelian', a reddish semi-precious stone.

Sarto

An Italian name from the Latin, 'mender'. An old occupational name like Barber.

Saul

From the Hebrew, 'asked for' or 'prayed for'. In the Bible he was the first king of Israel. St Paul was called Saul before his conversion to Christianity on the road to Damascus.

SHORT FORMS: Sol, Sollie, Solly.

Saville

Taken from the surname possibly meaning 'his town' in French.

OTHER FORM: Savile.

Sawyer

From the Old English, 'a sawer of wood'. An old occupational name.

SHORT FORM: Saw.

Saxon

From the Old German, 'knife'. The name of the tribe from Saxony who invaded England in the 5th and 6th centuries.

SHORT FORM: Saxe.

Sayer

From the Celtic, 'carpenter'.

Scipio

From the Latin, 'walking stick', this was the name of two great Roman generals.

Scott

A name meaning 'from Scotland', which is gaining in popularity in modern times.

OTHER FORMS: Scot, Scottie, Scotty.

Seabrook

From the Anglo-Saxon for a place where a stream runs into the sea.

Seamas

A modern Irish form of James.

OTHER FORM: Seamus.

Sean

Irish for John. The name became very popular due to the actor Sean Connery who played the character James Bond in several films.

OTHER FORMS: Shaughn, Shaun, Shawn, Shoon.

Seanan

A traditional Irish name from the Gaelic, 'old' or 'venerable'.

OTHER FORM: Senan.

Sebastian

From the Greek, 'venerable', Sebasta is the name of a town in Asia Minor. St Sebastian was a martyr who was shot by arrows and whose story has inspired many religious paintings.

SHORT FORMS: Seb, Sebbie.

Sebastien

French form of Sebastian.

Segel

From the Hebrew, 'treasures'. In the Bible the Israelites were known as the treasured people.

Selden

From the Old English, 'wonderful, rare'.

OTHER FORMS: Seldon, Don.

Selwyn

From the Old English, 'friend of the house', this name is found more often in Wales.

OTHER FORMS: Selwin, Win, Wyn.

Septimus

From the Latin, 'seventh'. Either a name for the seventh son or one born in the seventh month.

SHORT FORM: Sep.

Sergei

A Slav name from an old Russian family name. The 14th-century St Sergei is a popular Russian saint.

SHORT FORMS: Serge, Sergi.

Serle

From the Old German, 'armour', this was a fashionable Norman name.

Sergent

From the Old French, 'a military servant'.

OTHER FORMS: Sargent, Seargent.

Seth

From the Hebrew, 'appointed', in the Bible this was the name of Adam and Eve's third son. The Puritans favoured the name in the 17th century.

Seton

From the Old English, 'seaside town'.

Seumas

The Scottish Gaelic form of James.

Seumus
An old Irish Gaelic form of James.

Seward
From the Old English, 'defender of the sea'.

Sexton
An old name still used for the person who looks after the church fabric and its graveyard.

Sextus
From the Latin, 'sixth', used for children born on the sixth day or month or year, as well as the sixth son.

Seymour
From the Old English, 'sea' and 'marshland' or from the distinguished surname derived from St Maur in Normandy.
OTHER FORM: Seymore.

Shafiq
From the Arabic, 'kind, compassionate'.

Shahid
Arabic for 'witness' or 'martyr'.

Shahin
An Arabic name meaning 'falcon'.
OTHER FORM: Shaheen.

Shamir
From the Hebrew, 'diamond'. The tiny legendary creature was used to cut diamonds and the stones for Solomon's temple.

Shamus
A variation of Sean, the Irish form of James.

Shannon
A name taken from the Irish river and district, with the meaning 'old wise one'.

Shane
An Anglicized form of Sean.

Sharad
An Indian name from the word meaning 'autumn'.

Sharadchandra
An Indian name, a blend of the word meaning 'autumn' and the Sanskrit 'moon'.

Sharif
From the Arabic, 'eminent, honourable'. The title given to descendants of the Prophet Muhammad.

Sharman

Taken from the surname, from the Old English, 'to cut'.

OTHER FORMS: Shearman, Sherman.

Shaw

From the Old English, 'wood, copse', this first name is taken from the surname.

Sheldon

An English place name and surname used as a first name.

Shelley

Taken from the surname meaning 'meadow near a hill'. The poet Percy Bysshe Shelley made the name known.

Shem

A biblical name for one of Noah's sons.

Shep

A short form of Shepherd.

Shepherd

From the occupational name for a guardian of sheep.

OTHER FORMS: Shepard, Sheppy.

Sher

From the Persian, 'lion'. Sher Khan was the name given to the tiger by Rudyard Kipling in *The Jungle Book*.

Sheridan

From the surname which originally derived from Gaelic. The 18th-century Irish playwright Richard Brinsley Sheridan was a famous bearer of the name, as more recently is the actor, Sheridan Morley.

SHORT FORM: Sherry.

Sherlock

The name of the fictional detective Sherlock Holmes probably from the Old English, 'enclosed land'.

Sherman

From the Old English, 'sheep shearer'. Used in the US in honour of the famous Civil War general of the same name.

Sherwood

From the Old English, 'woodland'. Sherwood Forest was where the legendary Robin Hood robbed the rich to help the poor.

Shiva

From the Sanskrit, 'benign', this is the name of an important Hindu god. There are many names which add a suffix to this, such as Shivaji, with the meaning 'Lord Shiva'.

Sholto

From the Gaelic, 'sower', this is one of the names used by the Scottish Douglas family.

Shyam

From the Sanskrit, 'dark', this name is associated with the Hindu god Krishna.
OTHER FORM: Sham.

Sidney

Taken from the surname of the aristocratic family, which may have derived from the Old English, 'riverside meadow'.
SHORT FORMS: Sid, Syd.

Siegfried

From the Old German, 'peace after victory'. The name of the legendary Norse hero who fell in love with Brunhilde and was immortalised in Wagner's music.
SHORT FORMS: Sig, Siggie.

Sigfrid

A variation of Siegfried.

Siegmund

From the Old German, 'victory' and 'guardian'.
OTHER FORMS: Siegmond, Sigismund, Sigmund.

Silas

A short form of the Latin name Silvanus meaning 'wood'. He was a companion of St Paul on his journeys. It is also the name of two saints.

Silvester

From the Latin, 'of the woods'. Several early saints bore the name as did three popes.
OTHER FORMS: Silvan, Silvio.

Simeon

A biblical name from the Hebrew, 'he heard'. The name of the devout old man who blessed the child Jesus in the Temple.
OTHER FORMS: Shimone, Sim, Simi.

Simon

The English version of Simeon. Simon Peter was the chief of the Apostles of Jesus and there have been various saints with the name.
SHORT FORMS: Sim, Simmie.

Sinclair

Taken from a prevalent Scottish surname, which derived from the Norman French St Clair.

Sion

The Welsh form of John.

Sinbad
The story of Sinbad the Sailor comes from the Persian tales of 1001 Nights.

Siva
A variation of Shiva.

Siward
From the Old Germanic name meaning 'conquering guardian'.

Skelly
From the Gaelic, 'storyteller'.

Skipper
Originally a nickname for the captain of a ship, occasionally used as a first name.
SHORT FORMS: Skip, Skippy.

Slade
From the Anglo-Saxon, 'valley dweller', the name of a popular music group.

Snehin
From the Sanskrit, this has come to mean 'friend'.

Snowden
From the surname derived from Old English, 'snow shelter'.

Sol
From the Latin, 'sun'. Also a short form of Solomon.

Solomon
From the Hebrew, 'man of peace'. In the Bible he was a king of great wisdom.
SHORT FORMS: Sol, Solly.

Solon
From the Greek, 'wise man'.

Somerled
A Scottish name derived from the Norse 'summer traveller'.
OTHER FORM: Summerlad.

Somerset
A surname and an English county, meaning 'summer resting place'.

Somerton
A transferred surname from the Anglo-Saxon 'summer town'.

Somhairle
A Gaelic name from the Norse 'summer wanderer'.

Sorley
The Anglicized form of Somhairle.

Sorrell

From the Old French, 'light chestnut-brown', it is more often a girl's name.

Spalding

Derived from an English place name, this comes from the surname meaning 'split meadow'.

Spencer

Taken from the surname, recently popularised by Diana, Princess of Wales. It means 'steward' or 'butler'. More common as a first name in the US, where it is known through the filmstar Spencer Tracy.

Spike

Originally a nickname, but used as a first name, particularly in the US.

Spiro

A Greek name meaning 'breath of life'.

Squire

From the French, 'esquire' meaning a knight's attendant.

Srikant

From the Sanskrit, 'beautiful throat', which is a name connected with the Hindu god Shiva.

OTHER FORMS: Shrikant.

Stacy

A short form of Eustace.

Stafford

From the Old English, 'walking stick'. Sir Stafford Cripps was a British Labour politician.

OTHER FORM: Staffard.

Stamford

From the surname meaning 'stony ford'.

OTHER FORM: Stanford.

Stanislaus

From the Slav meaning 'glory of the camp'. The name of a well-known Polish saint, which has made it popular in Poland.

OTHER FORMS: Stan, Stanislav, Stanislaw.

Stanley

Taken from the surname meaning 'stony meadow', this was the name of the Conservative prime minister Sir Stanley Baldwin.

OTHER FORMS: Stan, Stanly.

Stefan

A European form of Stephen.

Steffan

A Welsh form of Stephen.

Stephen

From the Greek, 'crown' or 'garland'. St Stephen was the first Christian martyr and another saint of the name started the reformed Cistercian movement.
SHORT FORMS: Steve, Stevie.

Steven

A variation of Stephen.

Sterling

From the Old English, 'star', it has been the name of the British currency.

Stewart

From the Old English, 'steward', this is a name of the royal house of Scotland.
SHORT FORMS: Stew, Stu.

Stirling

A variation of Sterling, best known for the racing driver Stirling Moss.

Stoke

From the Middle English, 'village'.

Strahan

From the Gaelic, 'poet' or 'wise man'.

Stratford

From the Old English, 'street' and 'ford'. Stratford-on-Avon is the town where Shakespeare was born and where his plays are performed. Known through the television actor Stratford Johns.

Struther

From the Gaelic name meaning 'stream'.

Stuart

A variation of Stewart, introduced to Scotland by Mary Stuart, Queen of Scots.
SHORT FORMS: Stew, Stu.

Stuert

A variation of Stuart.

Sucat

From the Gaelic, 'warrior', this was St Patrick's baptismal name.

Suhayl

The Arabic name of one of the brightest stars in the southern constellation Carina.

Sujan

The Indian name meaning 'honest'.

Sullivan

From the Old English, 'field on the hill'.
SHORT FORMS: Sullie, Sully.

Sultan

From the Arabic, 'prince, ruler'.

Sunil

A modern usage from the Sanskrit, 'deep blue', sometimes associated with 'sapphire'.

Sunni

A short form of Surinder.

Suraj

An Indian name meaning 'the sun'.

Surinder

An Indian name, a variation of Indra, meaning 'mightiest of gods'.
Other form: Surendra.

Sven

From the Norse, 'boy', this is a mainly Swedish name.

Swain

From the Norse, 'attendant', in medieval times it came to mean a young country lover.

Sweeney

From the Gaelic name meaning 'little hero'.

Swithin

From the Old English, 'strong'. St Swithin was Bishop of Winchester in the 9th century
OTHER FORMS: Swithun.

Sylvester

A variation of Silvester.

Syril

A variation of Cyril.

T ~ Girls

Tabatha
Modern spelling of Tabitha

Tabitha
From the Aramaic, 'gazelle'. In the Bible she was a charitable woman who was restored to life by St Peter.
SHORT FORMS: Tab, Tabbie, Tabby.

Tacey
From the Latin, 'silent'. Also a variation of Tracey.

Takara
From the Japanese, 'precious'.

Talia
A short form of Natalie or a variation of Thalia.
OTHER FORM: Tally.

Talitha
From the Aramaic, 'little girl'.
OTHER FORM: Talia.

Tallulah
Taken from a Gaelic name meaning 'abundance' and 'lady'. Best known through the actress Tallulah Bankhead, although her name is said to come from a native American word for 'bubbling spring'.
OTHER FORM: Tallula.

Talya
A short form of Natalya.

Tamar
From the Arabic, 'date palm'. In the Bible Absolom's daughter 'of fair countenance', was named Tamar.

Tamara
The name of a Russian queen, probably derived from Tamar.
SHORT FORMS: Tammie, Tammy.

Tamarind
From the Arabic, 'Indian date palm'. This tree produces fruit which is used for chutneys and curries.

Tammy

A short form of Tamara and Tamsin, currently used in its own right. It was made known by a popular song of the same name, which was a bestselling record in the US.

Tamsin

A female form of Thomas, mainly found in the south-west of England.
OTHER FORMS: Tamsine, Tammy.

Tamzen

A variation of Tamsin.
OTHER FORM: Tamzin.

Tangerine

From the Anglo-Saxon, 'girl from Tangiers', this is also the name of the orange-like fruit.

Tania

A variation of Tanya.

Tanisha

Apparently a West African name from the Hausa tribe, which means 'girl born on Monday'. Used mainly in the US by Afro-Americans.
OTHER FORMS: Taneisha, Tanesha, Taniesha.

Tanith

The Phoenician goddess of love.
OTHER FORM: Tanit.

Tansy

From the French name of a wild flower of a yellow colour. Also a short form of Anastasia.

Tanya

The Russian pet form of Tatiana.

Tara

The name of the hill in County Meath, the seat of the ancient kings of Ireland. Used for the heroine, Tara King, in the television series *The Avengers*.
OTHER FORMS: Tarah, Tarra.

Taree

A first name found in Australia, probably from an aboriginal word for a fig tree.

Tasarla

An English gypsy name meaning 'morning' and also 'evening'.

Tasha

A short form of Natasha.

Tasnim

From the Arabic, 'paradise fountain'.
OTHER FORM: Tasneem.

Tatiana

St Tatiana was a Russian martyr honoured by the Orthodox church and was the name of one of the daughters of the last Tsar of Russia.

SHORT FORM: Tanya.

Tatum

A modern coinage, probably derived from an Old English place name. Best known for the film star Tatum O'Neal.

Tauba

From the German, 'dove'.

Tawny

Possibly from the colour of light brown hair, or from a Norman baronial name deriving from a place in France.

OTHER FORM: Tawney.

Taylor

From the French, 'to cut'. The name is derived from the surname taken from the occupation of a tailor. Most often found in the US.

Teal

The name of a type of wild duck, this is one of the modern girl's names taken from birds.

OTHER FORM: Teale.

Tecla

A variation of Thecla.

Teddy

A short form of Theodora.

Tegan

From the old Cornish, 'ornament' or the Welsh 'beautiful'.

Tegwen

From the Welsh, 'fair' or 'pretty'.

Tejal

An Indian name which means lustrous.

Tekla

A variation of Thecla.

Teleri

A Welsh name, an extension of Eleri.

Tellus

From the Latin, 'goddess of the earth'. Tellus Mater was the goddess of birth-giving.

Tempest

From the French, 'storm', another of the girl's names taken from the elements.

Tenecia

A variation of Tanisha.

Tenesha

A variation of Tanisha.
OTHER FORM: Tenisha.

Teresa

The Spanish form of Theresa. St Teresa of Avila was renowned in the 16th century and Mother Teresa of Calcutta was famous for her work with the poor in the 20th century.
SHORT FORMS: Terri, Tess, Tessa, Tessie.

Terri

A female form of Terry.
OTHER FORM: Teri.

Terryl

A modern combination of Terri and Cheryl.

Tertia

From the Latin, 'third'. The name given to the third daughter, or one born on the third day or month.

Tess

A short form of Tessa. Well known from the Thomas Hardy novel *Tess of the D'Urbervilles*.

Tessa

A short form of Theresa.
OTHER FORM: Tessie.

Tetty

An old pet form of Elizabeth.

Thalassa

From the Greek, 'sea', which gives its name to a salt water therapy much used in Mediterranean countries.

Thalia

From the Greek, 'to flourish'. She was one of the Three Graces who gave joy to men.

Thecla

From the Greek, 'God's glory'. It was the name of the first female martyr, St Thecla.
OTHER FORMS: Tecla, Tekla, Thekla.

Theda

A short form of Theodosia or Theodora. It was briefly popular in the US in the early 20th century due to the silent filmstar Theda Bara.

Thea

From the Greek, 'goddess', and a short form of names such as Alathea and Anthea.

Thelma

Possibly a short form of the Greek word meaning 'wish'. It has become more popular since the film *Thelma and Louise*.

Theo

A short form of Theodora, but used as a name by itself.

Theodora

The female form of Theodore which comes from the Greek, 'gift of God'.
OTHER FORMS: Thyra.

Theodosia

From the Greek, 'god' and 'giving', this was the name of several early saints.

Theophila

From the Greek, 'loved by God', this name was popular in the 17th century.

Theresa

Possibly from the Greek, 'to reap'. The name of the wife of the 5th-century St Paulinus, it did not arrive in Britain until the 18th century.
SHORT FORMS: Tess, Tessa, Tessie.

Thérèse

The French form of Theresa or Teresa.

Thessaly

A name taken from the region of eastern central Greece.

Thomasina

A female form of Thomas.
OTHER FORMS: Tamsin, Thomasine.

Thora

From the Norse, 'the thunderer' as Thor was the mythical god of thunder. Best known because of the actress Thora Hird.
OTHER FORM: Thyra.

Tia

A modern coinage taken from names ending in 'tia'.

Tiara

A modern name from the Greek, via Latin, meaning 'jewelled headdress'.

Tierney

From the Irish surname, used in the US as a girl's name.

Tiffany

An Anglicized form of the Greek 'God appears'. Traditionally a name for girls born on 6 January, the feast of the Epiphany. The name became popular during the late 20th century due to the film *Breakfast at Tiffany's*.

Tiegan
A variation of Tegan.

Tilly
A short form of Matilda.

Timothea
A rare female form of Timothy.

Tina
Taken from the diminutive of names ending in 'tina' such as Christina, it is now used as an independant name.

Tirzah
From the Hebrew, 'delight', this is a biblical name.
OTHER FORM: Tirza.

Tisha
A short form of Laetitia or Patricia.

Tita
A female form of Titus and a name formed from the ending of names such as Martita.

Titania
From the Greek, 'giantess' it is the name of the queen of the fairies, which Shakespeare used in his play *A Midsummer Night's Dream*.

Toba
A female form of Toby.

Toinette
A variation of Antoinette.

Toni
A short form of Antonia used in its own right.

Tonya
A short form of Antonia and a variation of Tanya.

Topaz
Derived from a gemstone. The topaz is usually yellow or brown.

Tori
From the Japanese meaning 'bird'.

Toria
A short form of Victoria.
OTHER FORM: Tory.

Tottie
A pet form of Charlotte, more common in the 18th and 19th centuries.
SHORT FORM: Totty.

Tourmaline
A rare name taken from the semi-precious stone.

Toyah

A variation of the invented Afro-American name, LaToyah. Best known for the actress Toyah Willcox.

Tracy

A very popular name probably derived from the surname which came from a place name in France.
OTHER FORMS: Tracie, Tracey.

Tricia

A short form of Patricia.

Trina

A short form of Katrina.

Triona

A short form of Catriona.

Trisha

A variation of Tricia.

Triss

A short form of Beatrice.

Trixie

A short form of Beatrice.

Trudi

A short form of Gertrude.
OTHER FORMS: Trudie, Trudy.

Tuesday

A name that can be given to a girl born on that day.

Tulasi

From the Sanskrit, 'sacred basil', this is the name of an Indian goddess.

Turquoise

From the French, 'Turkish stone'. A blue-green precious stone, long prized for jewellery.

Tybal

From the Old English, 'holy place'.

T ~ Boys

Tabor
From the Persian, 'drum'.
SHORT FORMS: Tab, Tabby.

Tad
A short form of Thaddeus used in the US as an independent name. Also the Anglicized form of Tadhg.

Tadhg
A traditional Gaelic name, meaning 'poet' or 'philosopher'.

Taffy
The Welsh form of David.

Tahir
From the Arabic, 'pure'.

Talbot
The surname of an old English family who gave their name to a breed of dog with a keen sense of smell.

Talcot
From the Old English, 'lakeside cottage'.

Taliesin
From the Welsh, 'shining brow', it was the name of a 6th-century Welsh poet and is now having a revival.

Tam
The Scottish short form of Thomas.

Tanner
Taken from the surname denoting a man who treated animal skins for leather.

Tariq
From the Arabic, 'nocturnal visitor'.

Tarlach
A modern short form of a traditional Irish name, which was the name of a high king of Ireland.

Taro
Japanese for 'big boy', traditionally given to the first-born son.

Tarquin
Probably of Etruscan origin this was the name of two early Roman kings.

Tarun
From the Sanskrit, 'young' or 'tender'.

Tate
From the Middle English, 'cheerful', this is derived from the surname.
OTHER FORM: Tait.

Taylor
From the Middle English surname meaning 'maker of clothes'. The first name is used in the US equally for boys and girls.

Taz
From the Middle English, 'pile' or 'heap'.

Teague
An Anglicized form of Tadhg.
OTHER FORM: Teigue.

Tearlach
A variation of Tarlach.

Ted
A short form of Edmund and Edward.
OTHER FORM: Teddy.

Tennyson
This name means 'son of Tenny (Denis)'. The poet Alfred Lord Tennyson made it known in the late 19th century.
SHORT FORMS: Tenn, Tenny.

Terence
Taken from the name of a noble Roman family, Terentius. The modern name came from Ireland, where it was used as the English form of Tarlach.
SHORT FORMS: Terry, Tel.

Terrance
A variation of Terence, most used in the US.
OTHER FORMS: Terance, Terrence.

Terrell
Taken from the surname and a variation of Tyrrell.

Terry
A short form of Terence.
OTHER FORM: Tel.

Tex
Originally a nickname for someone who came from Texas, now used in its own right.

Thaddeus
A biblical name of one of the minor Apostles. Possibly from the Greek, 'given by God'.
SHORT FORMS: Thad, Tad.

Theobald

From the Old German, 'bold people', the name was carried to Britain by the Normans.

SHORT FORM: Theo.

Theodore

From the Greek, 'gift of God', this was the name of many saints. It was popular in the US due to President Theodore Roosevelt who gave his name to the toy bear.

SHORT FORMS: Ted, Teddy, Theo.

Theodoric

From the Old German, 'ruler of the people'. The name was revived in 18th-century Britain, but is now rarely used.

OTHER FORMS: Terry, Theodric.

Theophilus

From the Greek, 'loved by God'.

SHORT FORM: Theo.

Thierry

French form of Terry.

Thomas

From the Aramaic, 'twin'. In the Bible Thomas was one of the 12 Apostles. There have been countless saints with this name, notably St Thomas-a-Becket.

SHORT FORMS: Tom, Tommy.

Thorn

A short form of Thornton.

Thornton

From the Old English, 'place of the thornbush', this name is associated with Thornton Wilder, the American writer.

Thurstan

From the Norse, 'Thor's stone', an old name that is still used in the north of England.

Tibor

From the Slavonic 'holy place.

Tiernan

From the Gaelic deriving from 'lord'.

Tierney

Taken from the Irish surname, derived from the Gaelic. St Tighearnach was the bishop of Clogher in the 6th century.

Tiger

From the striped jungle animal, denoting strength and beauty. Known through the American golfer Tiger Woods.

SHORT FORM: Tige.

Tilak

This Indian name is taken from the word for the caste-mark worn by Hindus.

Tilden

From the Old English, 'cultivated field'.
SHORT FORMS: Tildy, Tilly.

Tim

A short form of Timothy, also used independently.
OTHER FORM: Timmy.

Timon

The name of the hero of one of Shakespeare's plays, taken from a story by Plutarch.

Timothy

From the Greek, 'to honour God'. In the Bible it is the name of a companion of St Paul, who became bishop of Ephesus.
SHORT FORMS: Tim, Timmy.

Titus

Of unknown origin. The name of a Roman emperor and used by Shakespeare. Titus Oates was a 17th-century conspirator and it was the name of Mervyn Peake's hero of his Gormenghast novels.

Tobias

From the Greek, 'God is good'. The biblical story of Tobias and the angel made the name popular in medieval times. There was a 4th-century St Tobias.
OTHER FORMS: Tobiah, Tobey, Tobit.

Toby

The modern version of Tobias.
SHORT FORM: Tobe.

Todd

From the Middle English, 'fox', the first name was taken from the surname.
OTHER FORMS: Tod, Toddy.

Tolomey

A variation of Bartholomew.

Tom

A short form of Thomas, long used as an individual name.
OTHER FORM: Tommy.

Tonio

A short form of Antonio.

Tony

A short form of Anthony, used as a name in its own right.

Torcall

From the Norse, 'Thor's cauldron', this Gaelic name used in north Scotland.

Torquil

The Anglicized form of Torcall.

Townsend

From the Old English, 'edge of the town'.

Tracy

Taken from the surname of a noble French family or from the Latin, 'to manage'. This name is used for boys in the US, but is more common for girls.

Trahern

From the Welsh, 'strong as iron'.
Other form: Trahaearn.

Travis

From the French, 'to cross', this transferred surname is used regularly in Australia and the US.

Trefor

The Welsh form of Trevor.

Tremaine

From the Cornish place name meaning 'the house on the rock'.

Trent

From the name of an English river. Used mainly in the US.

Trenton

From the city in New Jersey named after the Quaker leader, William Trent, where the British were defeated in a battle during the American Revolution.
SHORT FORM: Trent.

Trevelyan

From the Cornish surname 'home of Elian'.

Trevor

From the Welsh, 'large homestead'. Popular in other parts of the world as well as Wales.
SHORT FORM: Trev.

Tristan

An old Celtic name of obscure origin, borne by the legendary romantic hero who loved Isolde. Their tragic story was used by many writers and notably by Richard Wagner in his opera Tristan and Isolde.
OTHER FORMS: Tristran.

Tristram

A variation of Tristan.

Troy

From the old city in Asia Minor besieged by the Greeks for many years. As a first name it is used mainly in the US and Australia.

Truman

From the Old English, 'trusty man'. Made famous by the US President Harry S. Truman.

Tucker

From the occupational name meaning 'cloth finisher'.
SHORT FORMS: Tuck, Tucky.

Tudor

A short form of Theodore or from the name of the English royal family in the 15th–17th centuries.

Tudur

From the Welsh meaning 'ruler of the tribe'.

Tulsi

From the Sanskrit, 'holy basil', a plant regarded as sacred to Vishnu.

Turlough

From the Irish Gaelic, 'instigator'.

Turner

From the Latin, meaning someone who turns wood on a lathe. Used as a first name in the US.

Tybalt

The medieval form of Theobald, used by Shakespeare in his play *Romeo and Juliet*.

Tyler

From the surname, meaning a person who covers roofs with tiles.
SHORT FORMS: Ty, Tye.

Tyree

From the name of an Irish county.

Tyrone

From the name of an Irish country. Sir Tyrone Guthrie was a well-known British theatre director.
SHORT FORM: Ty.

Tyrrell

Taken from the nickname of a stubborn person, from the French, 'to pull'.

Tyson

From the French, 'firebrand' and a nickname for a hot-tempered person. Mainly used in the US.
SHORT FORM: Ty.

U ~ Girls

Uda
From the Old German, 'prosperous'.

Ula
From the Old German, 'inheritor'.

Ulani
From the Hawaiian meaning 'bright' or 'lighthearted'.

Ulema
From the Arabic, 'learned, wise'.
OTHER FORM: Ulima.

Ulrica
From the German, 'powerful ruler', this is the female form of Ulric.

Ultima
From the Latin, 'final, greatest', a name for the last girl in the family.

Ulva
From the Old English, 'wolf', denoting courage.

Umeko
From the Japanese, 'plum-blossom'.

Una
From the Latin, 'one, unity'. The name was used in Irish legend and poetry and its Irish form may derive from the Gaelic, 'lamb'.
OTHER FORMS: Oona, Oonagh.

Undine
From the Latin, 'wave', this was the name of a mythical water spirit.
OTHER FORMS: Ondine, Undina.

Unice
A variation of Eunice.

Unity
From the Latin, 'one', this is one of the names taken from the virtues. Best known because of Unity Mitford, one of the famous Mitford family, who was an admirer of Adolf Hitler.

Urania
From the Greek, 'heaven', the name of
the Muse of Astronomy.

Ursula
From the Latin, 'female bear'. The name
of a 5th-century saint who was martyred
while on a pilgrimage in Germany. A
modern influence has been the filmstar
Ursula Andress.
SHORT FORMS: Urse, Ursie.

Uta
From the German, 'rich'.

U ~ Boys

Udell
From the Old English, 'yew-tree valley'.
OTHER FORMS: Udale, Udall.

Ulick
An Irish form of William.

Ulric
From the Old English, 'strong ruler'.
There was a 10th-century saint of the
name, St Ulric of Augsburg.
SHORT FORMS: Ric, Ricky, Ull.

Ulysses
Latin form of the Greek Odysseus, the
hero of Homer's epic poem. Used mainly
in the US due to President Ulysses S.
Grant

Umar
From the Arabic, 'flourishing', this was
the name of a good companion of the
Prophet Muhammad and is therefore
popular with Muslims.
OTHER FORM: Omar.

Umberto
From the Latin, 'umber', the colour of
earth. This mainly Italian name is known
through Umberto Ecco, the novelist.

Upton
Taken from the surname which derives
from the Old English, 'upper town'.

Uranus
From the Greek, 'heaven'. This is the
name of one of the seven planets.

Urban
From the Latin, 'one who lives in a
town'. This was the name of eight popes.

Uri
From the Hebrew, 'light' and a short
form of Uriah.

Uriah
In the Bible he was the husband of the
lovely Bathsheeba. Dickens used the
name for a cunning character in his
novel *David Copperfield*.
SHORT FORMS: Uri, Yuri.

Urien

A Welsh name possibly derived from the word for 'town'.

OTHER FORMS: Urian.

Usman

The Turkish form of Uthman.

OTHER FORMS: Osman.

Uthman

From the Arabic, 'bustard' (the bird), this was the name of a relative of the Prophet Muhammad. The word Ottoman, used for the empire of the Turks, derived from this.

V ~ Girls

Val
A short form of Valentine or Valerie.

Vala
From the German, 'the chosen one'.

Valda
From the Norse, 'ruler' or 'heroine of the battle'.

Val
A short form of Valentine or Valerie.

Vale
From the Latin, 'valley'.
OTHER FORM: Vail.

Valentina
A variation of Valentine.

Valentine
From the Latin, 'healthy, strong'. St Valentine's Day, 14 February, celebrates the 3rd-century saint and the pagan festival of spring, and is dedicated to lovers.
SHORT FORM: Val.

Valeria
A female form of Valerian.

Valerie
This is the French form of the Latin, 'to be strong', and originally came from a Roman family name.
SHORT FORMS: Val, Vallie.

Valeska
From the Russian, 'glorious ruler'.

Valetta
A fairly recent invention, probably an elaboration of Val. This is the name of the capital of Malta.
OTHER FORM: Valletta.

Valma
Of doubtful origin, but possibly from the Welsh 'mayflower'.

Valmai
Mainly used in Australia in the 20th century, this is probably an elaboration of Val.

Valonia

From the Latin for acorn-like fruit.
OTHER FORM: Vallonia.

Valory

A variation of Valerie.

Vanda

A variation of Wanda.

Vanessa

A name said to have been invented by
the 18th-century writer Jonathan Swift
for a friend of his called Esther
Vanhomrigh. Best known for the actress
Vanessa Redgrave.
SHORT FORMS: Nessa, Nessie, Vania,
Vannie.

Vania

A female form of Evan or Ivan.

Vanna

A short form of Giovanna.

Vanora

From the Celtic, 'white wave'.

Varda

From the Hebrew and the Arabic, 'rose'.

Varuna

An Indian name for the ancient god of
the waters who looks after the universe.

Vashti

From the Persian, 'beautiful'. In the
Bible she was the wife of a king of Persia.

Veda

From the Sanskrit, 'knowledge'. The
Vedas are a collection of sacred writings.

Vela

From the Latin, 'sail', this is the name of
a constellation in the Milky Way, seen in
the southern hemisphere.

Velda

From the German, 'field', implying
someone with special knowledge.

Velma

Possibly a short form of Wilhelmina, this
name appeared in the US in the late
20th century.

Velvet

Like Satin, a name taken from the
luxurious soft cloth

Venessa

A modern form of Vanessa.

Venetia
Derived from Venice, the beautiful city in Italy.
OTHER FORMS: Veneta, Venita, Vinita.

Ventura
From the Spanish, 'good fortune' or 'luck'.

Venus
The Roman goddess of love and the name of a planet. This is more usual among Afro-Americans.
SHORT FORMS: Ven, Vin, Vinny.

Vera
From the Latin, 'true'. This also comes from the Russian name meaning 'faith' and became popular in Britain in the 20th century.

Verbena
From the Latin, 'the sacred bough'. This is another name for vervain, a plant used to make a calming drink.

Verda
From the Latin meaning 'green, verdant'.

Verena
Probably derived from the Latin, 'truth', this name is found more often in Switzerland. It was borne by a 3rd-century saint who lived near Zurich as a hermit.
OTHER FORMS: Verene, Verina, Verita.

Verily
A variation of Verity.

Verity
One of the names of the virtues, this derives from the Latin, 'truth'. It was used by the 17th-century Puritans.

Verna
Of fairly recent coinage, proably a short form of Verena or Verona.

Verona
Taken from the name of the Italian city or a short form of Veronica.

Veronica
Derived from the Latin, 'true image'. The legend tells that St Veronica wiped Christ's face with a towel on his way to Calvary and an imprint was left on the cloth. She is the patron saint of photographers.
SHORT FORMS: Ronnie, Vera, Vonnie.

Véronique

The French form of Veronica.

Vespera

From the Greek, 'evening'. Vesper is the name of the evening star and vespers are evening prayers.

Vessa

A modern invention taken from Vanessa or Vesta.

Vesta

The name of the Roman goddess of fire and the hearth. It became known in Britain through the music-hall performer Vesta Tilley.

Veva

A short form of Genevieve.

Vevila

From the Gaelic, 'harmonious' or 'melodious'.

Vi

A short form of Violet or Vivien.

Vicky

A short form of Victoria.
OTHER FORMS: Vic, Vick, Vickie.

Victoria

From the Latin, 'victory'. Immensely popular following the reign of Queen Victoria, the name has become very fashionable again. The nickname Queenie is also used as a given name.
SHORT FORMS: Tori, Toria, Vic(k), Vicky.

Vida

A short form of Davida.

Vidonia

From the Portuguese, 'vine branch'.

Vigilia

From the Latin, 'alert, vigilant'.

Vignette

A diminutive of the French 'vine'.

Vijaya

From the Sanskrit, 'victory'. One of the names for the wife of Shiva.

Villette

From the French, 'small town'. Used in the 19th century after the name of the novel by Charlotte Brontë.

Vilma

A female form of William.

Vikki
A short form of Victoria.

Vina
From the Latin or French, 'wine', or a short form of Davina.

Viola
From the Latin, 'violet'. Used by Shakespeare for the heroine of his play *Twelfth Night*, this is the name of a flower of the pansy family. Is also a stringed musical instrument.

Violet
Taken from the name of the flower, usually of a deep purple colour. This was a popular name throughout the 19th century.
SHORT FORM: Vi.

Violetta
Italian form of Violet.

Violette
French form of Violet.

Virgilia
The female form of Virgil.

Virginia
From the name of a young Roman girl killed by her father to save her virtue. Sir Walter Raleigh named the state in America after Queen Elizabeth I, the 'virgin queen' and the first child born there was called Virginia.
SHORT FORMS: Gini, Ginny, Jinny.

Virginie
French form of Virginia.

Vishala
The female form of the Indian name Vishal, meaning 'immense'.

Vishalakshi
An Indian name meaning 'wide-eyed'.

Vita
From the Latin, 'life', this was invented in the 19th century. The most famous bearer of the name was the writer Vita Sackville-West. Also a pet form of Victoria.

Viti
A short form of Victoria.

Viv
A short form of Vivian or Vivien.

Vivi
A pet form of Vivian or Vivien.

Vivian
From the Latin, 'full of life', this was originally a boy's name but is now used for girls as well. There are many spellings for it.
SHORT FORMS: Viv, Vivi.

Vivien
The name of an enchantress in the legends of King Arthur, which may be a Celtic name derived from the Gaelic, 'white lady'.
SHORT FORMS: Viv, Vivi.

Vivienne
French form of Vivien.

Vivyan
A variation of Vivian.

Von
A short form of Yvonne.

Vonda
A variation of Wanda.

Vyvyan
A variation of Vivian.

V ~ Boys

Vadim
A short form of Vladimir.

Vail
From the Latin, 'valley'.
OTHER FORM: Vale.

Val
A short form of Perceval or Valentine.

Valerian
From the Latin, 'healthy', this is also the name of a medicinal herb, whose root is used as a stimulant.
OTHER FORMS: Valerius, Valery, Vallie.

Valentine
From the Latin, 'healthy' or 'strong'. The feast day of the 3rd-century martyr, St Valentine, is celebrated on 14 February and this has been amalgamated with the pagan fertility festival of spring to make it a day dedicated to lovers.
SHORT FORM: Val.

Van
The Dutch for 'of' or 'from' generally used as part of a surname. Also a short form of Evan or Ivan, used in its own right.

Vance
Mainly used in the US, this name is associated with the Anglo-Saxon for 'barn'.

Vane
From the Dutch 'of' or 'from'.
OTHER FORMS: Van, Vanne, Von.

Vaughan
From the Welsh, 'small'.
OTHER FORM: Vaughn.

Venn
From the Old English, 'handsome'.

Verdi
From the Latin, 'green'. Taken from the surname, best known for the Italian composer Giuseppi Verdi.
OTHER FORM: Verdo.

Vere

From the Latin, 'true' or 'faithful'. This name came from the aristocratic family name, which was brought to England by the Normans.

Vergil

A variation of Virgil.

Verney

From the Old French, 'alder'.

Vernon

From the Old French, 'alder grove', the name was taken from a Norman surname derived from various French placenames.

SHORT FORMS: Verne, Vernie.

Vibert

From the French, 'life' and the Old English, 'bright, shining'.

Vic

A short form of Victor.

Vidar

In Norse mythology he was one of the sons of Odin.

Victor

From the Latin, 'conqueror', the name became fashionable in the reign of Queen Victoria.

OTHER FORMS: Vic, Tiktor, Vittorio.

Vijay

From the Sanskrit, 'victory' or 'booty'.

Vikesh

An Indian name meaning 'the moon'.

Vikram

From the Sanskrit, 'stride' and also 'heroism', this is one of the names for the god Vishnu. Known through Vikram Seth, the Booker prize-winning novelist.

Vinay

From the Sanskrit, 'guidance' or 'training'. In Buddhist texts it implies the modesty required of monks.

Vincent

From the Latin, 'conquering'. The name of various early saints, including St Vincent de Paul, who founded a charitable order to help the poor, which still flourishes in Europe.

SHORT FORMS: Vince, Vinny.

Viral

An Indian name, which means 'priceless'.

Virgil

Associated with the Latin, 'stick' and therefore 'staff-bearer'. The name is given in honour of the famous 1st-century Roman poet, whose work has been translated by generations of schoolchildren. More usual in the US among Afro-Americans.

OTHER FORMS: Vergil, Virge, Virgy.

Vishal

An Indian name meaning 'immense' or 'spacious'.

Vishnu

The name of the Hindu god who is the personification of the sun.

Vittorio

The Italian form of Victor.

Vitus

From the Latin, 'lively'. St Vitus is the saint invoked to cure nervous complaints.

Vivian

From the Latin, 'alive, lively'. Although this was originally a boy's name it is now more often used for girls.

OTHER FORM: Vivien.

Vladimir

From the Slavonic, 'world prince'. Vladimir I was the first Christian ruler of Russia and was made a saint.

SHORT FORM: Vadim.

Vladislav

From the Slavonic, 'glorious ruler'.

Volney

From the Latin, 'to fly'.

Vyvyan

A variation of Vivian.

W ~ Girls

Wahiba
From the Arabic, 'generous giver'.

Walida
From the Arabic, 'new-born'.

Wallis
From the Old French, 'foreign' or 'stranger'. A name made famous by Mrs Wallis Simpson for whom Edward VIII gave up the throne.

Wanda
Possibly derived from the Norse, 'a slender stick', this name is found in 19th-century Polish folk stories. It is the title of a novel by the romantic writer Ouida.

Warrene
A female form of Warren.

Welcome
From the Old English, 'desired arrival'.

Wenda
A variation of Gwenda or Wendy.

Wendy
The name of Peter Pan's friend in the J. M. Barrie story, it was invented by the writer. Possibly from a lisped pronounciation of 'friend', or as a contracted form of Gwendoline.
OTHER FORM: Wendi.

Wenona
A variation of Winona.

Whitley
From the Old English, 'white clearing', this transferred surname is mainly used in the US.

Whitney
From the Middle English, 'by the white island'. Its vogue in the US probably derives from the singer Whitney Houston.

Wilfreda
A female form of Wilfred.

Wilhelmina

A female version of the German form of William.

SHORT FORMS: Mina, Minnie.

Willa

A female form of William.

Wilona

From the Old English, 'desired'.

Willow

Taken from the willow tree, implying pliant grace.

Wilma

A female form of William.

OTHER FORMS: Elma, Vilma.

Wilmette

A modern invention from the US, a diminutive of Wilma.

Winema

From a native American word meaning 'woman chief'.

Winifred

An Anglicized form of the Welsh Gwenfrewi, connected with the Old English, 'joy' and 'peace'. The name of an early saint, who miraculously came to life after being beheaded by a rejected lover.

SHORT FORMS: Win, Winnie, Freda.

Winifrid

A variation of Winifred.

Winnie

A short form of Edwina or Winifred.

Winona

An native American name, from the Sioux word 'first-born daughter'.

Winsom

From the word meaning 'pleasing' or 'attractive'.

Wren

One of the names taken from the names of birds.

Wynona

A variation of Winona.

Wynne

From the Celtic, 'fair maiden' or a variation of the short form of Winifred.

W- Boys

Wade
From the Old English, 'ford' or 'wade'. Wada was a legendary sea-giant.

Wagner
From the Dutch, 'waggoner'. One of the names derived from an occupation.

Wainwright
From the Old English, 'wagon-maker', this is a transferred surname.
SHORT FORMS: Wain, Wayne, Wright.

Wal
A short form of Wallace and Walter.

Walbert
From the Old English, 'strong wall'.
SHORT FORMS: Walber, Walby.

Waldo
From the Old German, 'ruler'. The first name is used mainly in the US and is known through the writer Ralph Waldo Emerson.

Walker
From the Old English, 'to tread', an occupational name for a fuller of cloth, which became a surname.

Wallace
From the Old French, 'foreign' or 'stranger', it was used by the Welsh and northern Britons. Its use as a first name started in Scotland due to William Wallace, the great 13th-century patriot.
SHORT FORMS: Wal, Wall, Wally.

Wallis
A variation of Wallace used in the US for boys and girls.

Walter
From the Old German name meaning 'army ruler'. Well known through Sir Walter Raleigh, who first introduced tobacco to Elizabethan England.
SHORT FORMS: Wal, Wally, Wat, Walt.

Walt
A short form of Walter, used in its own right particularly in the US.

Warburton
From the Anglo-Saxon, 'castle town'.

Waqar
From the Arabic, 'dignity' or 'sobreity'.

Ward
From the Old English, 'guardian' or 'watchman'.

Warner
From the Old German, 'guard' and 'army', the name was brought to Britain by the Normans.

Warren
Partly from the Old German, 'guard' and also from the French place name meaning 'game park'. The actor Warren Mitchell is a recent bearer of the first name..
SHORT FORMS: Warr, Warry.

Warwick
The name of a town in the British Midlands, probably derived from the Old English, 'farm by the dam'. The Earl of Warwick fought on both sides in the 15th-century Wars of the Roses.
SHORT FORM: Warrie.

Wasim
From the Arabic, 'graceful, handsome'.

Washington
From the Old English place name meaning 'Wassa's town'. Particularly used in the US because of the first president George Washington, whose family came from the village of Washington in Northumberland.

Waverley
From the Anglo-Saxon, 'aspen tree' and 'meadow'.
OTHER FORM: Waverly.

Wat
A short form of Walter.

Watkin
The diminutive of Wat or the transferred surname.

Wayland
From the Old English, 'land by the path'.

Wayne
From the Old English, 'cart', this surname came from a cart maker. Its popularity as a first name was largely due to the American filmstar John Wayne.

Webster
From the Old English, 'weaver', mainly used as a first name in the US.
SHORT FORMS: Web, Webb.

Wellington

Either from the Old English, 'well' or 'willow' and the Gaelic, 'hill-fort'. The famous Duke took his title from the English place name.

Wenceslas

The name of the king in the Christmas carol comes from the Slavic, 'greater glory'.

Wendell

From the German, 'Vandal'. It became known as a first name in the US due to its use by the Wendell Holmes family.

Wesley

Taken from the surname with the Old English meaning 'western meadow'. John and Charles Wesley were the founders of the Methodist Church, but the first name is not now necessarily chosen for religious reasons.

SHORT FORM: Wes.

Weston

From the Old English, 'west settlement'. A transferred place name and surname.

Whitney

From the place name meaning 'by the white island'. It use as a first name in the US is probably due to it being the surname of a wealthy patron of the arts.

Wilber

From the Old English, 'well' or 'willow' and 'bright'. More common in the US.

Wilberforce

From the surname taken from the Old English, 'Wilburg's ditch'. The first name was given in honour of the 19th-century anti-slavery campaigner William Wilberforce .

Wilbur

A variation of Wilber. Best known for the successful novelist Wilbur Smith.

Wilfred

A variation of Wilfrid.

Wilfrid

From the Old English, 'desire for peace'. There were two early saints with the name, one of whom was the Bishop of York in the 7th century. The name was revived in the 19th century.

SHORT FORM: Wilf.

Wilhelm

The German form of William.

Willard

From the Old English, 'resolute and hardy'. Mainly used as a first name in the southern US.

William

From the Old German, 'resolute protection'. This has always been a very popular name, even though it was that of the Norman Conqueror of England. It has many royal connections and was also the playwright Shakespeare's first name.
SHORT FORMS: Bill, Billy, Will, Willie.

Willoughby

From the Old English, 'house by willow trees'.

Wilmer

From the German, 'resolute and famous'.

Wilmot

From the German, 'of resolute mind'.

Wilson

The surname means 'son of Will'. Used as a first name in the US in honour of President Woodrow Wilson.

Wilton

From the Anglo-Saxon, 'the farm by the well'. The name comes from a town in England famous for wool carpets.

Windsor

The surname of the British royal family, and also a town in Berkshire.

Wingate

From the Anglo-Saxon, 'winding lane'.

Winston

The surname comes from the name of a small Gloucestershire village. The first Winston Churchill was given his mother's surname in 1620 and it has been in the Churchill family ever since. Popular as a first name in honour of the great 20th-century statesman.
SHORT FORMS: Win, Winnie.

Winter

This is a suitable choice for a boy born during the winter months.

Winthrop

The name of various places in England. This is more common in the US in honour of the Winthrop family who were colonial governors of New England.

Winton

From the Old English, 'Win's settlement'.

Witt

From the Old English, 'fair' or 'white'.

Wolfe

From the German, 'wolf', meaning a brave man.
OTHER FORMS: Wolf, Wulf.

Wolfgang

From the German, 'wolf path'. This was one of the names of the composer Mozart.

SHORT FORMS: Wolfe, Wolfie.

Woodrow

From the Anglo-Saxon, 'hedge in a wood'. Used as a first name in honour of the American President Woodrow Wilson.

Woody

A short form of Woodrow, best known for the comic filmstar Woody Allen.

Worcester

The name of a city in the British Midlands, possibly meaning 'the camp amongst the alder trees'.

OTHER FORM: Wooster.

Wordsworth

Used mainly in the US the first name is given in honour of the poet William Wordsworth.

Worth

From the Old English, 'enclosure', this is part of many English place names. The first name may also be used to imply someone who is 'worthy'.

Wyatt

From the Old English, 'war' and 'hardy', this is taken from the surname. Best known for Wyatt Earp, the American gambler who fought at the OK Corral.

Wycliffe

From the Norse, 'village near the cliff'.

Wyn

From the Welsh, 'white' or 'blessed'. Since the Middle Ages it has been popular in Wales.

Wyndham

Taken from the place name meaning 'Wigmund's homestead'. John Wyndham was a 20th-century science fiction writer.

Wynne

A variation of Wyn.

Wystan

From the Old English name 'battle stone', this was the name of a 9th-century saint. Rare in modern times it is known through the poet Wystan Hugh Auden.

XYZ ~ Girls

Xanthe
From the Greek, 'yellow'.
OTHER FORM: Xantha.

Xanthippe
From the Greek, 'yellow horse'. This was the name of the wife of Socrates.

Xaverine
A female form of Xavier.

Xavia
A female form of Xavier.

Xaviera
A female form of Xavier.

Xara
A variation of Zara.

Xena
A variation of Xenia.

Xenia
From the Greek, 'hospitality', taken from the word for a stranger.

Ximenia
From the botanical name of tropical herbs named after a Spanish missionary, Ximenes.

Xylia
From the Greek, 'wood'.

Xylophila
From the Greek, 'wood' and 'love'.

Yakira
From the Hebrew, 'precious'.

Yardena
A female form of Jordan.

Yarkona
From the Hebrew, 'green', this name comes from a bird which has yellow-green feathers.

Yasmin
From the Persian word for the sweetly scented flower, more commonly known as Jasmine.

Yasmina
A variation of Yasmin.
OTHER FORM: Yasmine.

Yelena
A variation of Helena.

Yetta
A short form of Henrietta.

Ynez
A variation of Ines or of Agnes.

Yoko
From the Japanese, 'female' 'positive'. A name known through John Lennon's wife, Yoko Ono.

Yolanda
Probably derived from the Greek, 'violet', it is also a variation of Iolanthe.

Yolande
The French form of Yolanda.

Yosepha
A variation of Josephine.

Ysabel
A variation of Isabel.

Ysanne
A combination of Yseult and Anne.

Yseult
The French form of Isolda.
OTHER FORM: Yseulte.

Yvette
The female form of Yves.

Yvonne
From the French, 'yew'

Yuki
From the Japanese, 'snow' or 'lucky'.

Yulan
From the Chinese, 'jade orchid', the name of a magnolia tree.

Zabrina
A variation of Sabrina.

Zahra
From the Arabic, 'flower' or 'shining'. The name is given in honour of the mother of the Prophet Muhammad.

Zainab
A variation of Zaynab.

Zakiya
From the Arabic, 'pure, virtuous'.
OTHER FORMS: Zakiyah, Zakiyya.

Zamira

From the Hebrew, 'song'.

Zandra

A variation of Sandra.

Zanna

A modern variation of Susanna.

Zara

The Anglicized form of Zahra. It became popular when the daughter of Princess Anne, the Princess Royal, was given the name.

Zaylie

Probably a version of the French Célie or Zélie.

Zaynab

The name of several members of the family of the Prophet Muhammad, probably derived from the name of a sweet-smelling plant.

OTHER FORMS: Zeinab.

Zea

From the Latin, 'ripe grain'.

Zelah

From the Hebrew, 'side'. In the Bible it is the name of one of the 14 tribes of Israel.

Zelda

A variation of Griselda. Best known through the wife of the writer F. Scott Fitzgerald.

Zelia

From the Hebrew, 'zealous' or 'ardent'. Also a variation of Celia.

Zelma

A variation of Selma.

Zena

Possibly from the Persian for 'woman', or a short form of Zinaida.

Zenith

From the Arabic, 'path over the head' meaning the highest point.

Zenobia

From the Greek Zeus and 'life'. Queen Zenobia of Palmyra was a powerful ruler in the 3rd century. The name was used in Cornwall in the 16th century.

Zephyr

From the Greek, 'the west wind', implying someone soft and gentle.

Zephyrine

A French name from the Greek, 'west wind'.

Zerlina

From the German, 'serene beauty'.
OTHER FORMS: Zerline, Zerla.

Zeta

From the Hebrew, 'olive'.

Zillah

From the Hebrew, 'shade'. In the Bible
she appears in the Book of Genesis and
the name is used by modern Israelis.
OTHER FORM: Zilla.

Zina

A Russian short form of Zinaida or
Zinovia.

Zinaida

From the name of the Greek god Zeus.
It is the name of two obscure Russian
saints.

Zinnia

From the name of the brightly coloured
tropical flowers.

Zinovia

A Russian variation of Zenobia.

Zipporah

From the Hebrew, 'bird'. In the Bible it
is the name of the wife of Moses.

Zita

Probably from the Italian for 'a girl'. St
Zita is the patron saint of servants.

Zoë

From the Greek, 'life'. The name was
used by the early Christians.
OTHER FORM: Zoe.

Zola

A modern creation possibly influenced
by the surname of the French novelist
Emile Zola.

Zsa-Zsa

A pet form of Susan, associated with the
Hungarian filmstar Zsa-Zsa Gabor.
OTHER FORMS: Zaza.

Zula

A modern invention taken from the
Zulu tribe of southern Africa.

Zuleika

From the Arabic, 'beautiful' 'fair'. The
novel *Zuleika Dobson* is about a girl at
Oxford who is so beautiful that male
undergraduates kill themselves for love.
OTHER FORM: Zulekha.

Zulema

From the Arabic, 'peace'.
OTHER FORM: Suleima.

XYZ ~ Boys

Xan
A short form of Alexander.

Xander
A short form of Alexander.

Xanthus
One of the names of the Greek god Apollo.

Xavier
From the surname of St Francis Xavier, who was one of the founders of the Jesuits in the 16th century. Its use as a first name is mainly found in Catholic families.
OTHER FORMS: Javier, Zavier.

Xenophon
From the Greek, 'stranger's voice'. The name of a 4th-cemtruy BC Greek army commander.
SHORT FORMS: Zeno, Zinnie.

Xerxes
From the Persian, 'king'. Xerxes I was king of Persia in the 5th century BC.

Xylon
From the Greek, 'wood' or 'forest'.

Yacub
A biblical variation of Jacob.

Yale
From the Old English, 'old'.

Yank
Possibly from the Dutch for John. The name was given to settlers in New England and later became a nickname for Americans.
OTHER FORMS: Yancy, Yankee.

Yardley
From the Old English, 'enclosed meadow'.

Yasin
An Arabic name from two letters at the start of one of the chapters of the Koran.

Yasir
From the Arabic, 'rich' or 'soft'.

Yehudi

From the Hebrew, 'praise'. Yehuda was part of King Solomon's kingdom. The most famous bearer of the name was the violinist Sir Yehudi Menuhin.

Ynyr

A Welsh traditional name of obscure origin, possibly meaning 'honour'.

Yorath

An Anglicized form of the Welsh name Iorwerth.

Yorick

From the Danish form of George, Jorick. Shakespeare used the name in *Hamlet*.

York

From the surname and the city in north-east England.

Yule

A name for someone born at Christmas. Yule was the pagan mid-winter feast.
OTHER FORMS: Yules.

Yusuf

A variation of Joseph.

Yves

A French form of the Welsh name Evan. The 14th-century St Yves came from the region of Brittany in France.

Zachariah

From the Hebrew, 'God has remembered'. In the Bible he was the father of John the Baptist. The Puritans used the name in the 17th century and through them it became known in the US.
OTHER FORMS: Zacchaeus, Zacharias.

Zachary

A variation of Zachariah. Best known in the US through President Zachary Taylor.
SHORT FORMS: Zac, Zack, Zak.

Zack

A short form of Zacary.

Zahid

From the Arabic, 'abstinent'

Zak

A short form of Isaac or Zachary.

Zake

Arabic for 'pure' or 'chaste'.

Zakki
A variation of Zachary.

Zamir
From the Hebrew, 'song', relating to the nightingale's song.

Zane
Taken from the surname, this became known as a first name through the American writer, Zane Grey.

Zavier
A variation of Xavier

Zeb
A short form of Zebedee or Zebulon.

Zebedee
From the Hebrew, 'Jehovah's gift'. In the Bible he was the father of the Apostles James and John.
SHORT FORMS: Zeb, Dee.

Zebulon
From the Hebrew, 'to exalt' or 'to dwell'. In the Bible he was the founder of one of the 12 tribes of Israel.
OTHER FORM: Zebulun.

Zechariah
A variation of Zachariah and Zachary.

Zed
A short form of Zedekiah, mainly used in the US.

Zedekiah
From the Hebrew, 'God's justice'. In the Bible there are three people with this name.
SHORT FORM: Zed.

Zeke
A short form of Ekekiel.

Zeus
From the Greek, 'brightness', this is the name of the supreme god in Greek mythology.

Zev
From the Hebrew, 'wolf', this is a popular name with Jewish parents.

Zion
A variation of Sion, the name of the hill on which Jerusalem was built, and therefore 'the promised land'.

Zola
From the German, 'toll' or 'price'. Known because of the French writer Emile Zola, this is more often a girl's name.
OTHER FORMS: Zoilo, Zollie.

Saints

Aiden	Basil	Constantine
Alexis	Benedict	Cornelius
Aloysius	Bernard	Cosmo
Ambrose	Bernadette	Crispin
Adrian	Boris	Crispian
Alban	Brendan	Cuthbert
Agatha	Brice	Cyril
Agnes	Bridget	Cyrus
Anastasia	Cadoc	Damian
Andrew	Candida	David
Angela	Casimir	Delphinus
Anne	Cathal	Dennis
Anthony	Cecilia	Deirbhile
Audrey	Chad	Dewi
Augustine	Christopher	Diego
Aurelius	Clare	Dominic
Barbara	Clement	Donnan
Barnabas	Columba	Dorothea
Bartholomew	Comhghall	Dunstan

Dymphna	Gertrude	Jocelyn
Edan	Gervase	Jude
Edith	Gilbert	Julia
Edmund	Giles	Julian
Edwin	Gobnat	Justin
Egbert	Godfrey	Katherine
Elmo	Godric	Kentigern
Eulalia	Gregory	Kevin
Eustace	Harvey	Kieran
Fabiola	Helen	Killian
Fatima	Helena	Knute
Felicity	Herbert	Lambert
Felix	Hilary	Laura
Ferdinand	Hilda	Laurence
Fergus	Hildebrand	Leonard
Fillan	Hubert	Lorcan
Finbar	Hugh	Louise
Flavia	Imelda	Lucia
Florian	Isidore	Lucilla
Francis	Ita	Lucy
Gall	James	Ludmilla
Gemma	Jerome	Luke
Genevieve	Joan	Magdalene
George	Jodoc	Magnus
Georgia	John	Marcella
Germaine	Joseph	Marcia

Margaret	Otto	Stephen
Marina	Patrick	Swithin
Mark	Paul	Tatiana
Marmaduke	Paula	Terence
Martin	Pelagia	Teresa
Mary	Peregrine	Thecla
Matthew	Peter	Theodore
Maura	Petronilla	Theodosia
Maurice	Philip	Thomas
Maximilian	Pius	Tobias
Melanie	Quentin	Ulric
Michael	Raymond	Ursula
Mildred	Regina	Valentine
Monica	Richard	Verena
Morwenna	Ronan	Veronica
Myron	Rowan	Vincent
Natalya	Sabina	Vitus
Nicholas	Samson	Vladimir
Ninian	Sarah	Wilfrid
Norbert	Sebastian	Wystan
Odile	Serge	Yves
Odo	Silas	Zachary
Olaf	Silvester	Zena
Olga	Silvia	Zita
Osmund	Simon	
Osyth	Stanislav	